Home, School and I
Towards an Understanding of Religious Diversity in School

Home, School and Faith:
Towards an Understanding of Religious Diversity in School

David W. Rose
MA, BD, Dip.Ed., ALBC

David Fulton Publishers
London

Published in association with the Roehampton Institute

David Fulton Publishers Ltd
2 Barbon Close, London WC1N 3JX

First published in Great Britain by
David Fulton Publishers 1992

Note: The right of David Rose to be identified as the author of this work has been asserted by him in accordance with the Copyright, Designs and Patents Act 1988.

Copyright © David Rose

British Library Cataloguing in Publication Data
A catalogue record for this book is available from the British Library

ISBN 1-85346-179-2

All rights reserved. No part of this publication may be reproduced, stored in a retrieval system or transmitted, in any form, or by any means, electronic, mechanical, photocopying, recording or otherwise, without the prior permission of the publishers.

Typeset by Chapterhouse, Formby, L37 3PX
Printed in Great Britain by BPCC Wheatons Ltd. Exeter

Contents

Foreword
David Crispin vii

Acknowledgements viii

1 Introduction 1

2 Names and Naming Ceremonies 5

3 Diet and Food as a Religious Symbol 19

4 Appearance and Clothing Linked to Religion 34

5 Language, Sacred Writings and Religion 46

6 The Calendar and Religious Festivals 58

7 Customs, Courtesies and Sacred Objects 73

8 Non-theistic Stances and Christian Sects 83

9 Conclusion 89

Glossary 91

Index 98

Foreword

The current market for RE textbooks would seem, at first glance, to be brimming over. Teachers and students of religion are able to select from an endless supply of texts which enable them to extend their own knowledge as well as help others in their understanding and awareness.

This book will be a valuable addition to those bookshelves as it offers something quite different and is very needed at this point in the development of Religious Education. It will also provide a means by which students of religion can develop mutual understanding and respect both for, and between, those of different religions as well as those without religious belief.

Its strengths lie in two important aspects. Firstly, the constant references made to real people from different faith communities. This gives the reader an insight into how religion actually works out in practice, and will help the reader to discern between the usual textbook ideas and the actual faith practices. Secondly, the classroom teacher is also given valuable advice in dealing with different issues as they arise with their students. Sensitivity is the key word used and with this clearly in mind a teacher should be able to develop ideas based on a variety of sources and traditions. This hopefully will lead pupils towards a greater knowledge and understanding of religion as well as an increased sensitivity towards the beliefs, practices and philosophies they expound. In this way the concepts, skills and attitudes learnt and acquired should enable the learner to approach religious people with sensitivity, understanding and respect based on accurate information and not on generalised stereotypes or ignorance.

It has been a learning experience to read this book in draft form. Knowledge of the author has also helped, as a great deal of research and experience is reflected on every page.

David Crispin
Advisory Teacher for Religious Education
London Borough of Sutton

Acknowledgements

This book is the result of a joint effort by a wide variety of people who have worked with me and supported me in this venture.

First and foremost my thanks go to my wife Gill who has positively encouraged me throughout. Without her support this book would not have come to fruition. She has put up with me typing for many hours of the day as well as reading the various drafts. She has encouraged me to visit and talk at length with those listed below.

My thanks go to David Crispin for initially reading and commenting helpfully on ways of improving the end product and then agreeing to write a foreword.

My thanks also go to Jim Docking who showed great patience and encouragement when it was most needed, as well as suggesting ways in which the text could be improved.

My profound thanks go to a great number of people who have encouraged me by their patience in answering many questions that must have appeared to them most trivial yet of great importance to me in writing this book. They also assisted with a range of follow-up questions when I have not totally understood the initial response. I have deliberately placed the following in alphabetical order because they have all given of their time and expertise to help me learn about their Faith.

> David and Anne Clarke,
> Phrah Dit,
> Mr. and Mrs. Masood Qureshi,
> Mr. and Mrs. Ratnasingham,
> Satpal Singh,
> Giani Ajit Singh,
> Phramaha Term,
> Mr. Ubhi, and many others older and younger at the Khalsa Centre, Tooting,

Sr. Meg Walshe,
John White,
Father Mike Yannatos

My thanks must also go to various students at the Roehampton Institute of Higher Education who encouraged this book through their search for clarity and understanding in my lectures.

D. W. Rose
January 1992

CHAPTER 1

Introduction

The aims of this book are quite straightforward though varied. The Education Reform Act 1988 requires

> a balanced and broadly based curriculum which –
> (a) promotes the spiritual, moral, cultural, mental and physical development of pupils at the school and of society; and
> (b) prepares such pupils for the opportunities, responsibilities and experiences of adult life. (Section 1(2))

Further, the Act requires religious education in schools to

> reflect the fact that the religious traditions in Great Britain are in the main Christian whilst taking account of the teaching and practices of the other principal religions represented in Great Britain. (Section 8(3))

The Elton Report (1989) on school discipline states

> we recommend that Headteachers and staff should work to create a school climate which values all cultures, in particular those represented in it, through its academic and affective curricula. (Section 6.63)

This book is an attempt to assist the teacher in the classroom to think positively about the requirements of law and the recommendations of others for an inclusive approach to our children in school. Amongst the religions considered are those of Buddhism, Christianity, Hinduism, Islam, Judaism and Sikhism.

It would be inappropriate to include a section in each chapter on non-theistic stances for living. Many of our pupils in the county school come from families where there is an absence of faith in a religious sense, yet will maintain clearly discernible codes of conduct and belief systems. An additional section at the end of the book is therefore included to assist understanding in this area.

The contents should prove to be a simple reference point for the way children's religious backgrounds can impinge on the school and classroom context. This book should not, however, be regarded as a general introduction to different Faiths. The reader should read books written by members of the Faith communities in order to understand the detailed nature of the religion being considered.

The particulars contained in this book have been discussed with members of the Faith groups represented. The attempt has thus been made to produce authenticity whilst trying to break down some of the stereotypes which often appear in text-books on religions and religious education. The book is designed as a starting point that hopefully will further enable the process of dialogue between Faith communities and teachers and other interested groups. It should enable individuals to develop their understanding of the impact of religion in society and answer some of the simpler questions which arise within the school context.

This book does not pretend to be definitive in its scope and content. The reader should bear in mind that within each Faith there are diversities of opinion and perspective. It should therefore be noted that diversity of home background means that there is a great danger in oversimplifying that which is exceedingly complex. Furthermore minority Faiths within the UK have had to face, and continue to face, the challenge of Westernising influences. Some have remained isolated, others have adopted and adapted, while others have felt strong enough within their own community to bring up their children with both Eastern and Westernising influences being syncretised. For some of the first generation of immigrants, the place from which they emigrated has altered drastically in terms of society and influences for change. The natural focus for their identity and roots will be found within the religious or believing community. The second and third generations of many minority religious groups are considerably different from those who immigrated into the UK within the past few decades. They may well be virtually Westernised by influence and often in practice, whilst the older people in the Faith community will often assume a more dominant role in maintaining the 'traditional' values. The result of these influences for change is that Faith is rarely static and a great variety of interpretations of practice are to be found exercised within the UK today.

It follows therefore that for most statements made about particular Faiths, there will be found devout members of that Faith who will claim to have a differing belief and style of life to that stated in this book. Hopefully this will not nullify the general validity of the material which has been selected, but it does highlight the difficulties when writing about other peoples' beliefs, ethical codes of conduct and practical expressions of that Faith. It also raises the contentious areas of nominality and pious devotion to a Faith.

This book will not attempt to analyse the different categories of family groupings except to emphasise that family patterns vary. The extended family is of central importance in the Indian sub-continent, whilst the nuclear family is more common within the Western nations. Within the extended family the concepts of responsibility and family obligation are therefore maintained even within and from the UK. Parental responsibilities and caring for the elderly are expected duties. For example if an older relative in India or East Africa is taken ill it is common for family members in the UK to go, at short notice, and care for them even for long periods of time. The nature of the family unit itself will thus have practical implications for children in school. The issue of mixed marriages has not been dealt with at all.

The contemporary classroom in many county schools, especially in urban areas, is rather complex in religious terms. Religion, far from 'dying' has far more diverse forms and expressions than the average person realises. A book such as this cannot possibly consider some of the more obscure or localised developments but a section on Jehovah Witnesses is briefly included in Chapter 8. Also built into that chapter is a section on non-theistic stances for living and how they might affect the classroom. Humanism has been used as the exemplar for this position.

A certain amount of terminology may be unfamiliar to the reader, but a simple glossary of religious terms used in the text is provided at the end of the book. These terms are highlighted in italic type within the main body of the text.

This book has distinctive categories and themes which are developed Faith by Faith. Where it is necessary, broader categories of information have been included so that the reader has a context in which to weigh up the comments included. There is therefore a linking of the Faith to home, school and the broader Faith community itself.

The Central Statistical Office publication *Social Trends 19* (1988) reveals that about 50 per cent of the UK born ethnic minority population is under the age of 10. Less than 7 per cent are over the age of 25. These two simple statements show the need for a book such as this which is designed to help the teacher in school.

In researching for this book I have had my own understanding challenged. This has been a rewarding experience because it has meant that dialogue has taken place and will continue. Hopefully in the interests of mutual understanding and co-operation the need for dialogue will become your experience as well.

CHAPTER 2

Names and Naming Ceremonies

It would not be an exaggeration to state that to take away someone's name is to dehumanise and lessen the true identity of that individual. Indeed, to give a criminal a number rather than a name is seen as a punitive aspect of the penal system.

Within the educational system it is considered desirable that all children should be treated with human dignity, yet often the issue of children's names is trivialised. The class register with the plethora of names it contains, is often a constant challenge for the teacher since some names are awkward to pronounce. Yet the attitude adopted towards achieving successful pronunciation reflects much about classroom practitioners and their attitude towards others. How we approach children has a direct bearing on their dignity and self-identity and ultimately on ours as the teachers.

The term *rite of passage* is usually given to those major stages in life ranging from birth, through initiation and marriage to death. It is not without significance that ceremonial rites accompanying birth and naming of the baby are universally present. Some are simple ceremonies, others more complex. Yet across all cultures the actual naming of a child is seen as of great importance. Many who would not term themselves religious do on these occasions seek to have some form of naming rite and on these occasions they usually involve a believing community, as for instance, in the Christian baptism ceremony.

In the UK there are many forms and occasions whereby individuals will be asked to state their 'Christian' names. Teachers need to be aware that this may well be inappropriate in a multi-cultural school context since it would be demeaning to those from a background other than Christian. To illustrate the point, I well remember a TV serial based on the work of an animal inspector. The inspector asks of a turbaned man, 'What is your Christian name?' It was no surprise that the man did not reply!

This chapter seeks to heighten awareness of the importance of names by considering names and naming rites from a variety of traditions. Western style and Eastern style naming patterns vary somewhat and for a variety of reasons. In general there are three Asian naming systems reflecting the three principal religious groups, namely Hindus, Sikhs and Muslims. Westernising influences and legal requirements, however, have altered practice somewhat so that the British naming system is often used in official records of Asians.

Buddhist birth and naming ceremonies

For the Buddhist family the surname will be the family name, though this can in practice change. Some surnames will have meaning but not necessarily of religious significance. The religious significance in Buddhist names rests in the manner in which the name is chosen.

The wife will usually adopt the husband's family name on marriage as in Western traditions. There are occasions, however, when family names have been combined at marriage. For example the paternal name Dum (which means 'black') may be combined with the maternal name of Deang (meaning 'red') to give the surname Dumdeang.

There is usually only one personal name and for this to be auspicious it will reflect consultation with the monks as well as astrological influences. This reflects the nature of Buddhism.

Some text books describe Buddhist birth and naming rites in quite elaborate and exotic terms. For some Buddhists there are these complex ceremonies. For example, the oldest members of the family prepare the cradle and clothes for the baby. Tools and books may be placed in the cradle of a boy, whilst needles and thread may be placed in the cradle of a girl. After the birth, the umbilical cord may be packed in salt and buried in a pot under two coconut trees. Yet when I discussed this with one Thai monk he declared he had never heard of the practice. No doubt, though, other monks and lay-Buddhists will have done. It is therefore worth remembering that rites and practices vary enormously from region to region, let alone from country to country.

It is, however, common practice that when a Buddhist baby is about one month old its head will be shaved. This is basically a matter of cleanliness. Sacred threads will be placed around the wrists as a welcome to *Khwan*, which is the spirit that will look after the baby. It is felt that if Khwan left the baby then it would be susceptible to illness and unhappiness.

The head shaving usually takes place in the presence of the Buddhist monastic community called the *Sangha*. The baby will be blessed with sacred water. It is fairly common practice that only a lock of hair will be cut off the baby rather than the whole head being shaved. This will be performed by the senior monk present. Some parents will wait until a later stage for this part of the rite especially if the child has little or no hair. If the baby is male he will be held by the monk for the blessing, if it is a girl she will be held by the parents. This reflects the practice of monks not to have physical contact with the opposite sex. The monks, or *Bhikkus* as they are called, consult the horoscope and decide on the lucky name for the child. Additionally there is significance in the day of the week on which this occurs. As there are 33 letters in the Pali alphabet and 44 in the Thai alphabet which are then further sub-divided, there are no shortages of options from which to choose.

The parents will choose the number of monks they wish to attend this ritual. It may be three, five or nine. Many parents almost as a matter of superstition, prefer the whole Sangha to be present. This seems to have arisen because of a word-play on Thai. The number nine in Thai is 'coa', the same spelling but different tone for 'coa' means 'step forward'. Through practice the concept of progress, expressed by 'coa', has been incorporated into this birth ritual with a preferred nine monks in attendance.

During this ceremony, attended by members of the family as well as the parents, there will be a chanting by the monks to wish the child a happy life. The whole occasion will last about half an hour.

Christian birth and naming ceremonies

The cultural heritage within most of Western Europe, including the UK is Christian. This is reflected in most stratas of society whereby there is the linking of State and Church. Within the UK the monarch is the titular head of the Church of England. In other ways too the state church is still influential within our system of government. For instance, whether one is Christian or not we all live within a 'parish' and as such have certain legal and ecclesiastical entitlements. As with most Faiths, however, it is a reality to have claimants to that Faith who do not practice it at any level. The phrase 'nominal Christian' represents a distinct category from those who are practising and believing Christians. The linking of State and Church means that nominality features heavily within the UK. The remarks which follow are intended to refer to those Christians who actively practice their Faith.

Infant baptism or *Christening* is the most popular form of birth rite celebrated in the majority of Christian churches. It is the occasion when the child is given a 'Christian' name. The 'Christian' names chosen by parents for their children may reflect personal preferences on the part of the parents; they may also reflect a positive choice of a name which is 'Biblical', as distinct from those with no Christian connotations. In this sense many Christian names are Jewish in their origins and names overlap within these two Faiths. Other common Christian names will be those of key historical Christian figures such as certain Saints. Many parents will check the meaning of the names chosen for their child although this is not a commonly practised criteria.

Christening is a sacramental rite which admits the candidate to the Christian Church. A sacrament is an action which is meritorious before God although it is commonly described simply as a rite.

The Christening occurs in Church and involves parents and godparents who all make promises to God about the way they will help bring up the child in the Christian Faith. The godparents or 'sponsors' will make the promises of renunciation, faith and obedience in the child's name. *Chism*, (an oil) and the holy water are used to draw the sign of the cross on the forehead of the child. The water may be poured over the head of the baby using a scallop shell or equivalent design. The child is then given its 'Christian' name. A candle may be lit and given to the godparent symbolising the presence of God. It is not uncommon in the Roman Catholic Church for a child to be given an additional name when he/she is confirmed later in life. This name, which will not appear on any legal documentation, is a personal choice and often reflects key figures within the Christian Faith, such as saints.

The Christening event may be celebrated afterwards at home with a party for family and close friends. Traditionally, silver gifts are given as presents. The Christening cake may well be the top tier of the parents' wedding cake.

It is not unusual for an adult who has never been Christened as a baby, yet who wishes to be confirmed as a member of the Christian Church, to participate in a Christening ceremony that leads straight on to confirmation.

Mention must be made of those *Nonconformist denominations*, such as the Baptists, whose members reject infant baptism. They tend to adopt an alternative practice such as a dedication or thanksgiving ceremony. This takes place shortly after birth and the use of water is avoided. These Nonconformists usually practice adult baptism (commonly called 'believers baptism') so that the individual being baptised is old enough to understand that the meaning of the action has implications for the style of life to be adopted subsequently.

Hindu names and naming ceremonies

For most Hindus born in the UK the naming system is quite straightforward. There may well be one or two personal names followed by the surname. The surname for Hindus may well be a sub-*caste* name borne by other members of the family. Traditionally it may reflect the name of a grandparent or great grandparent. In common with British practice, wives and children increasingly take their husband's or father's surname. Many Hindu families in Britain may well drop the traditional middle name. For those who keep records of peoples' names, such as a local education authority or other official bodies, it is almost always wrong to record a Hindu middle name as a surname.

The population of the Indian sub-continent is expected to top a billion by the turn of the century so it is little wonder that there are literally dozens of common Hindu sub-caste names and the naming becomes more complex. Some names are more popular in certain areas of India and will be linked to the deity worshipped locally. There are also variant naming patterns dependent on where in the Indian or African sub-continents the Hindus come from originally. In the UK perhaps the most famous family name, or sub-caste name, is Patel which is a Gujurati caste name meaning 'farmer'. There are dozens of other common sub-caste names such as Amin, Gupta, Parekh and Shah.

Within schools in the UK there will be some Hindu children who have the same surname as their parents whilst there will also be those with different surnames but similar initials to their parents. This reflects an ongoing Westernising influence which is virtually becoming the norm. Examples of common boys' names include: Anand, Anil, Gopal, Govind, Kapil, Ravi. Common girls' names include Indira, Jyoti, Meena, Nandita, but there are thousands of other popular names for both boys and girls.

Occasionally titles may be used before the names

Shri = Mr., Shrimati = Mrs.

Less frequently used female titles include Devi (literally means Goddess), and Wati or Kumari (literally means Princess). In Britain it is usually acceptable to use the titles Mr. and Mrs. If in doubt it is best to ask.

The first letters of a person's name will, for many, be the same as those of father/grandfather even if the surname differs. For example:

    Grandfather = Arumugam Thamar Sinnathura
    Father = Arumugam Thamar Sinnathura Nataraj
    Son = Thamar Sinnathura Navaratnasingham

With successive generations the first names tend to be omitted otherwise the name will become too lengthy. However the practice now for children being born in the UK is to adopt the father's surname and retain it. Time will tell whether this will become the established practice in the West.

The first name for many Hindus will be linked to the deity they worship. There are thousands of deities recognised within Hinduism and it is likely that various gods will be worshipped within a family and even more variations within a congregation at a Temple. For example devotees of the deity Ganesh may give their children associated derivative names, such as Ghanapathy or Vinayagar. The warrior God, Murgha has associated names, examples of which are Subramaniam, Velan, Kantha, Vedaivel or Arumugam.

At birth the baby is washed and the syllable Om written on the tongue with a golden pen dipped in honey. This is the norm in India though not always practised in the UK. Om is the holiest Hindu name for God showing He is Absolute. The person who performs this rite on the tongue may adopt the role of the godparent to the child, though not every family will have godparents. The parents tell the priest the exact date and time of the birth from which a horoscope will be prepared. Great importance is placed on symbolism within Hinduism including the use of numbers. For example, the number nine is an infinite number and is of great symbolic significance. There are nine planets which are considered to be of vital importance when naming a child, and the religious name given to a baby is based on astrological factors.

The *Brahmin*, or priest, suggests suitable syllables and sounds to the parents after which the child will be named. The priest will use his own idol from which to suggest the letter or sound for the baby's name. The parents may then ask the priest to suggest a name from the 1008 associated with their own deity or they might choose their own name for the baby. Naming usually occurs 10 to 12 days after birth, though increasingly in the UK the child may be named whilst the mother and baby are still in hospital following the birth. In some areas especially India the child is placed over and under a swinging cradle, once for each name. Women sing lullabies and special food 'prasadam' is eaten. However this is not so common in the UK, Mrs. Ratnasingham from the Ghanapathy Temple, Wimbledon, commented that this ritual was not performed for her children and that she had only ever seen it occur 'in the films'.

At the naming ceremony parents give presents and sweets to the family and friends. The child will be taken to the Temple after the first month of its life. Until that time all members of the family (including blood relatives) refrain from attending the Temple. After the end of the first month the family will usually book a ceremony called *Abishekam* where the deity is bathed and prayers are offered. This is a longer form of service, a shorter service called *artanai* at which the names are recited is quite popular.

Most Hindu ceremonies involve the help of the Brahmin. In many forms of traditional Hinduism there are sixteen samskaras or stages that are associated with the birth of a child. The first three occur prior to the birth and include the mother praying that the child will be healthy etc. Other stages include the occasion when the baby has solid food for the first time (samskara 7), when the ears are pierced (samskara 8), and when the head of the baby is being shaved. This latter samskara symbolises a clean, fresh start to life. Although this is usually practised when the child is one year old the timing may vary, with some families delaying until the child is three to four years old. This stage is often accompanied by a family party.

Names and naming ceremonies in Islam

Muslim names are fairly complex. A child may have three or four official names and also a personal name. This may mean that a child's first name is not the name by which he or she is to be addressed. The teacher should therefore ascertain what is the personal name of the child so that confusion and offence will not occur.

Whilst one can suppose the more common personal names will all have their origins in the Qur'an or from within the Islamic Faith, this is not necessarily a factor. Generally personal names reflect hope or aspirations for the child so-named. That these qualities are attributed to Allah means that similar names may occur universally within the

Muslim community. For example, the personal name Masood means 'noble'. This was an expression of the feelings of the child's parents when he was given the name, reflecting the desire for this quality to be present when the child had grown up. The name Shahid means 'clever', the name Jamil means 'beautiful'. So most Muslim families will choose names they like, which reflect their hopes for their children and these by derivation reflect the character of God.

Formerly, a common Arab practice was that a boy would be called iban, which means 'son of'. So for example, Jamil iban Masood is a name which reflects that Jamil's father is called Masood. However the Westernising influence of the past 200 years means that most families will have adopted a surname before living in the UK. Most families will have a surname, although it need not be the last name. For practical reasons (such as obtaining a passport) families settling in the West will make it the surname.

In some families all the male members may take a similar family name, for example Mohammed. Surnames generally have no real meaning or religious significance. Some from the Indian sub-continent may reflect their origins as a caste name. It is not unusual for the surname Patel or Chaudury to be a Muslim family name as well as a Hindu name.

Whilst not common, it is not rare for members of the same family to have completely different names, in cases where there is no family name/surname. For this reason it would be possible, though not usual, for two boys in the same class not to be easily identifiable as brothers.

There are differing naming systems in various parts of the Muslim world. Muslims from the Middle East will vary from those originating in Asia or parts of Africa. This should cause no problems in terms of registering a child at school.

Muslim birth rites are based on custom rather than religion because they are not prescribed within the sacred Qur'an. As a result customs vary from region to region. Many text-books give the impression that there is a common rite but this is misleading.

As a matter of course the baby will be bathed shortly after birth. Often the father says *Azan* (*Adhan*) in both the ears of the child. This is practised whether the baby is a boy or girl. This is the declaration of the unity of Allah and that Muhammad is His prophet. In some parts of the world, such as Pakistan, a ceremony called *Tahneek* occurs. This is when sugar or honey is placed in the mouth of the baby by an older family member. This custom is fairly unusual in the UK.

When the baby is one week old the *Aqeeqah* ceremony will be performed by most families. This is when the head of the baby is totally shaved and a gift of meat is given to friends and the poor. Some text-books refer to the equivalent of the child's hair-weight being given in silver to the poor, though this would be unusual. Whilst most families will practise charity to the poor at this stage, not all families will shave the head of the child. I met one Muslim family with three children who said that none of their offspring were shaved as it makes the subsequent growth of the child's hair coarse. These people also told me of some families who had their children's hair shaved totally on three occasions during infancy. The time of choosing the name of the baby and the moment of naming varies from family to family. Some choose before birth, others at some point during the child's first year.

It is common that *Khitan* or circumcision of the male babies will occur shortly after birth whilst the baby is a few days old. This is performed by the doctors at the hospital. In Turkey I have witnessed this rite being performed on boys aged 8-9 years old and this appears to be normal practice. Whenever it occurs it is usually prior to the onset of puberty. After it has taken place there is usually a celebration with family and friends.

Jewish names and naming ceremonies

The names given to Jewish children will vary in number, but each name will have particular significance besides being simply an English name. There will always be a Hebrew and/or a Yiddish name. This name will usually be used in the Hebrew school and the synagogue. The English name will be that which usually occurs on the register of a county school. Sometimes the Hebrew and English names will sound alike, sometimes not. Since all the names will have special meanings, it comes as no surprise that most Jewish children will also have a nickname.

As a general principle the Jewish names chosen will be traditional, Biblical names, based on the *Torah*, but if contemporary the name will have a Hebrew or Yiddish equivalent. Names chosen could include a parent's name, reflect the time of the year, or simply perpetuate the family traditions.

The names that are chosen for a child follow certain criteria. The parents may choose a name that reflects an idea, so if a daughter is born near to the Festival of Purim, she may be called Esther after the heroine of the story. Similarly birds or other natural things may be used as a basis of choice, Yonah, from which Anne is derived, means 'dove', while Deborah is derived from the term meaning 'bee'. The precedent for these types of names is found in the Torah.

Esau and Jacob in the Torah were given names symbolic to their birth. Esau means 'hairy' because the child had reddish hair at birth, Jacob the younger twin held his brother's heel, and so was named 'grabber'. The term 'heel' has passed into the English vernacular as a byword for a person regarded with contempt or disapproval.

Jewish choice of names usually perpetuates the family tradition. *Askenazi* Jews who originate from central and Eastern Europe, perpetuate the name of a recently deceased family member, often the grandparent or other close relative. It is only recently in Europe that Jews have given their children the name of a living relative. The traditional reason for not doing this in the past was that when the *angel of death* came for the relative they might be confused and take the wrong person. The *Sephardic* Jews, who originated from the Iberian peninsular in the fifteenth century, tend to choose the name of a close relative, whether they be living or dead.

There are usually two parts to the child's first names:

    boy's name(s) + son of father
    girl's name(s) + daughter of mother

For example, David and Anne have two children, a boy and a girl; the son is named Michael Ben David + surname. Michael is the grandfather's name, thus, with David perpetuating the family name. It is likely that when Michael has a son of his own that the baby boy will be named, David Ben Michael + surname. The term 'Ben' simply means 'son of'.

David and Anne have a daughter Esther Bat Anne + surname. Esther is chosen because it is Hebrew and Biblical and the daughter was born on the festival date of Purim. She has also taken her mother's name, Anne. When Esther has her own daughter it may be that she will be called after her grandmother, Anne Bat Esther + surname. Bat simply means 'daughter of'.

If the baby is a girl, then on the first *Shabbat* (sabbath) after her birth, the father announces the name in the synagogue and a special prayer is said. If the baby is a boy, *Brit Milah* or circumcision occurs at eight days old. This will take place at home. A chair is used which is called the 'throne of Elijah'. The baby will be held by the *Sandek* the Jewish equivalent of a godfather. The actual circumcision operation is performed by the *Mohel*, a trained circumciser. A blessing is said followed by *Kiddush* (a glass of wine that symbolises the sanctification of the day). A special party is held called *Seudat Mitzvah* (though this term literally means 'festive meal around a commandment', and therefore can occur on other occasions).

It is a relatively recent phenomenon for European Jews to have surnames. Traditionally they were called by their first names and their parents' names or a name related to their occupation. Many of these surnames associated with an occupation have now become accepted as family surnames in their own right. So for example Kaufman means 'merchant', Zimmerman means 'carpenter', Becker means 'Baker'. Sometimes surnames denote where a person has originated from, as Lubavich, a town in Russia, or Pollack which means Poland, or Weinburg which means 'a hill of grape vines'. (For further information the reader is encouraged to look at the Jewish Kids Catalog.)

Sikh names and naming ceremonies

Usually, but not always, Sikh names have three parts.

(1) The personal name is the name selected via the ceremony in the Gurdwara. The personal name for Sikhs is equivalent to the Christian name in Western Christian naming patterns. These names are equally applicable to boys and girls. This reflects the teaching of *Guru Gobind Singh Dev* who instructed this practice to show that everyone belongs to the same family. The names of Sikhs and Hindus are linked historically, and there is therefore an overlap between Hindu and Sikh personal names. Some personal names can be linked with Sikhs from the Punjab.

(2) The name *Singh* is usually added to a boy, whilst *Kaur* is usually added to a girl's name. From the school register Sikhs are therefore easily recognisable by the title Singh or Kaur. Singh means 'lion' and is given to all males. Kaur means 'princess' and is given to all females whether single or married. This title is usually positioned after the first personal name. These names may well be the only clue as to the sex of the child, since the other names could be given to a boy or a girl. It is not that unusual for some children to be given only their first name + the family name with the religious names Singh/Kaur omitted.

(3) The last name is the family name. Historically this is a sub-caste

name, derived from the Hindu origins with its complex caste system. More commonly today the name may reflect the village from which the family originates. In many instances this sub-caste name may be dropped. The dropping of the family surname, which indicates the caste background and origins, corresponds to the basic doctrinal belief that all people are equal before God. However many Sikhs in the UK are returning to using their hereditary family name and following the practices of the host country. On marriage a woman may assume her husband's sub-caste name only if he uses it. In other instances the family name will be derived not from the sub-caste name, but from the village of origin in India or the Punjab. For example those from the village of Gandran carry the surname Jittlar, whilst those from Plahi will have the name Sagoo. This is now the more common practice.

The following examples may help illustrate the alternative styles of addressing Sikh adults:

Surjeet Singh Khalsi   Surjeet Kaur Khalsi
Amarjit Singh Kahlon   Kuldip Kaur Kahlon

If the family sub-caste surnames are used adults would be addressed respectively as Mr. Khalsi or Mrs. Khalsi, Mr. Kahlon or Mrs. Kahlon. If not the first two names are used. Thus parents of Sikh children in the classroom may, for example, be addressed as Mr. Surjeet Singh or Mrs. Kuldip Kaur. Only those families that use their family name would be addressed as Mr. Khalsi or Mrs. Kahlon. It may be advisable to enquire of parents how they wished to be addressed rather than presume or run the risk of stereotyping. It is acceptable with children to use their first name only e.g. Surjeet, Amarjit or Kuldip.

The term 'Path' may be given to the reading out loud of the Sikh sacred scriptures. This may be called an *Akhand Path* if it is a non-stop reading which takes three days to complete, or it could be the *Sahaj Path* that is completed over a longer period of time such as a week. The Sikh scriptures are called the *Guru Granth Sahib*. They are treated literally as the living words of God and so are given a resting place or bedroom at the *Gurdwara* or temple. Only if a family has a spare bedroom may members have their own copy of the Guru Granth Sahib in their home. So the 'Path' readings more commonly will occur at the Gurdwara.

Prior to the birth of a baby readings from the sacred scriptures may be said aloud as a 'Path' is performed. The reason lying behind this practice is the positive belief that the foetus will gain knowledge within the womb which will help the child to draw closer to God after birth.

Some Sikhs will visit the Gurdwara shortly after the birth of the baby to thank God for the gift of the child. There are no restrictions as to when this may occur nor who can attend. The mother and child will visit the Gurdwara when they feel ready to do so. Some Sikhs will announce the name during a service whilst others will choose not to.

On the occasion when a name is being chosen, a reading from the Guru Granth Sahib will be said at the Gurdwara. This will include the words of the *Mool Mantra* which is the central credal statement of faith, declaring the nature of God. Amrit, or honey, is usually placed on the tongue of the baby. Parents will have brought with them flour, sugar and ghee to make *Karah Prasad* which will be shared with others in the congregation. Parents may donate sweets for the occasion or possibly provide the *langar* or common meal. The parents may also bring a *Rumalah* as a gift. The Rumalah is an elegant cloth which is always used to cover the sacred writings when not being read.

When the baby is named the family will gather round Guru Granth Sahib. *Amrit*, or sweetened holy water, may be stirred with the *Khanda* sword and prayers said. A *kirpan*, or small dagger, may be dipped in Amrit and a drop placed on the tongue of the baby. The mother may drink the rest. The *Granthi*, the attendant priest, will open the Guru Granth Sahib at random. He will look for the point at which the heading appears on the page. He does not simply select the first letter at the top of the left page or the first letter of the next paragraph. If it is in the morning when the event is occurring, then the heading will be selected from the left hand page; if it is in the afternoon then the heading will be selected from the right hand page. The first letter of the heading thus randomly selected will be the first letter of the name of the baby. A variety of prayers may be said with equality being displayed in the sharing of the Karah Prasad. At this occasion the baby will be given the *Kara*, the bracelet. This is the first of what are called the 5 K's, which are the external symbols of a Sikh. This matter is dealt with in a later chapter.

Practical implications for a teacher

In concluding this chapter, what are the professional implications for teachers in the classroom?

- It is not a sign of weakness to admit to parents when we are uncertain or anxious about matters relating to Faith backgrounds. Indeed this type of open and honest approach will assist dialogue between home and school. The teacher will reveal a sensitive and earnest desire not to offend and at the same time will show a respect for the home and background of the individual child and the parents.
- Do not presume to guess or stereotype. Very many names extend across at least two Faiths, so there is a need to ascertain individual backgrounds.
- Whilst I can write a chapter on names and their possible religious significance, it should be remembered that there are levels of significance for names within any Faith. Some parents will choose an apparently 'religious' name simply because they like it and would not stress its deeper religious significance. Others may consciously choose the name because it reflects the traditions of the Faith community and may therefore be expected of them by the community or wider family. Yet others may choose the name because of its symbolic nature which reflects their own piety as well as reflect their aspirations for their child.
- There is a need for accuracy in addressing a child correctly. Backgrounds of children vary enormously, and there is an onus on teachers to ascertain the correct form of address in order to enhance the dignity of the individual child.

CHAPTER 3

Diet and Food as a Religious Symbol

In recent years many LEAs have exercised increasing sensitivity towards the dietary requirements of religious minority groups as well as beginning to provide for a greater range of religious groups and their dietary requirements. This reflects the broader changes taking place within society where the Faith communities will now increasingly have their own food suppliers and outlets for the purchase of 'permitted' foods. This coincides with the numerical increase of religious minorities within school. This has brought a challenge to the education system, and where a school is experiencing practical difficulties it would be wise to contact the home to ascertain specific needs.

A practical emphasis reflecting the importance and value of human relationships should help towards developing an atmosphere of mutual understanding, respect and trust. These qualities are the basis for sound dialogue. This takes time and effort on the part of the school but really reflects the ethos of a school. Most schools produce handbooks containing statements about the way individual children are considered. The Education Reform Act as well as the majority of Agreed Syllabuses for religious education reinforce the need for a broad-based understanding of religions and religious practices. The area of diet, however is one that needs to be accommodated further.

Buddhism and diet

It is interesting that most Buddhists are vegetarian since this is not what was taught by the Buddha. According to Pramaha Term at the Buddhapadipa Temple, Wimbledon, there is no textual basis for vegetarianism within Buddhism. The practice probably developed because Buddhism has a strong practical emphasis on mindfulness. This is part of the *Noble Eightfold Path* adopted as an ethical guide to daily living by the Buddhist. For some, right mindfulness would be interpreted in such a way that as the eating of meat involves the killing of the animal it is therefore wrong.

Another perspective on mindfulness is reflected in the factual statement that when an animal dies it has no life or feeling and therefore has become material which decays. The purity of that food for eating is therefore dependent on the mind of the individual. The Buddha taught that the individual should be mindful to have food and be moderate in actions. This allows the approach of vegetarianism as well as that of the carnivore.

The *bhikkus* or Buddhist monks are not allowed to work for monetary gain. Their role is a spiritual one and in return for their spiritual advice, example and teaching the lay-community will look after their needs for food. Monks, who receive food gifts from lay-people are commonly described in books as 'begging', though that is to misinterpret the esteem with which the lay-Buddhists respect and care for the monks and express this through daily food gifts. It would be less derogatory and more accurate to express this as 'collecting alms' in their bowl. The actions are different from those which many Westerners would describe as begging. The lay-people will give voluntarily because they wish to. The monk therefore has no say in the nature of the food they receive. In accordance with Buddhist teaching they will eat that which they are given, which may include gifts of meat. As most lay-Buddhists are in practice non-meat eaters it follows that most monks will be also. Vegetarianism is not intrinsically bound up with their religious beliefs, and the distinction needs to be understood.

For both monks and lay-Buddhists, food practices in a Buddhist country such as Thailand differ greatly from those in the UK. In Thailand, with both bowl and body covered, the monk will accept food from anyone by standing in front of their house. They will wait for up to three minutes before moving on. In the UK this is not practised. The lay-Buddhist community, in the UK, will bring their food gifts to the Temple or monastery itself. The food may be given to the *Sangha* or passed directly to the cook. The monk will eat his food before midday.

There is no religious significance to the layout of a typical Buddhist kitchen either in the temple or in the home. Whilst in some traditions food is of great symbolic significance and associated with certain festivals, the same cannot be said of Buddhism. This may be a result of Buddhist emphasis on the 'spiritual' rather than the temporal realm. However, Buddhist festivals do involve food at two main levels. Usually the lay community will bring gifts of food to the sangha particularly at festival time. Secondly, food will feature as part of shared eating either within the family or within the communal gatherings of the local community, though this is not symbolic as in many religions.

Christianity and diet

There are no general rules relating to diet that affect all Christians. Preferences for certain diets may reflect personal choice rather than general beliefs. Some Christians would stress that the Creation story in Genesis chapter 1 is a foundation for vegetarianism. Others argue that the incident of *Peter's Vision* in the New Testament (recorded in Acts chapter 10) abolishes any earlier dietary requirements and that all foods are permissible. St. Paul in writing to the Christians at Corinth (1 Corinthians 10) appears to leave it as a matter of conscience for the individual Christian.

Most Christians believe that food comes from God and acknowledge this by giving thanks (or saying *grace*) before a meal. For many Christians this is further developed in practical terms by giving to Christian charities which care for the relief of others. Examples of two 'large' Christian charities are Christian Aid and Tear Fund. Caring for others is often left to individual discretion although some churches require their members to practise tithing. This latter form of giving is normally linked to the maintenance of that church rather than charitable acts.

A tradition exists today of not eating meat on Friday, and in many public and Christian homes fish is customarily served instead. This was formally a requirement on those who were Catholic but was abolished after the Second Vatican Council in the 1960s, being linked with the practice of penance. Prior to Vatican II there was greater emphasis on the corporate identity of the Catholic Church. Subsequently the emphasis has shifted to the individual's right to a choice of action in this matter of eating fish on a Friday. The reasons for this practice seem to vary. Some claim it marks and respects the fact that Jesus died on a Friday. Others see it as linked to the historical Christian practice of fasting and days of abstinence. Yet others would emphasise that the symbol of the fish is representative of the Christian Church and the practice of eating fish on one day of the week reflects this perspective. Whatever the reasons, there are still many schools, institutions and establishments that traditionally provide fish on Fridays.

Fasting is a fairly common practice within certain Christian denominations but is not heavily emphasised nor practised today by the majority of Christians. However it was a widespread practice in Judaism, taught by John the Baptist and Jesus, and commonly practised by the early Church. Although in recent years it has not been heavily emphasised by Christian Churches, perhaps the closest to a general fasting is the period of *Lent*. Originally this was only a two day fast, but it has now been extended to forty days. Apart from Lent many Christians linked to 'high' Church will not have anything to eat on a Sunday before they have attended Mass. This in reality has meant a day's fast timed from the previous midnight.

Food as a Christian symbol is included in the service of what the Church of England would call Holy Communion or the *Eucharist*. Catholics, including the Orthodox Church, would call the same rite the Mass, whilst the Nonconformist may well refer to it as the Lord's Supper or Breaking of Bread. Whilst there are differences in interpretation as to the meaning of the rite, the overall emphasis is the same. Christians meeting together will take some bread, or something comparable such as a wafer, symbolising the body of Jesus, and, they will also take some wine symbolising the fact that in dying Jesus shed his life-blood vicariously (that is, as an innocent being punished so that the guilty may be pardoned). Christians celebrate the Eucharist in remembrance of Jesus' death.

Increasingly some Christians are practising an Agape feast. This 'love' feast is expressed by individuals giving and sharing food together. This corporate act often culminates in an eucharistic act. This type of meal is referred to by St. Paul in I Corinthians 11 when he is correcting malpractice and alludes to the practice incidentally.

In all religions food is inextricably bound up with festivals, and this is true within Christianity, especially in the period around Lent and Christmas.

The day prior to Lent is called Shrove Tuesday. It is a time of rejoicing and in many countries there is a time of Carnival. This is especially true to the Christian communities in the Caribbean, and increasingly so in the black-led churches in the UK. It is a day when all rich foods are eaten prior to the period of Lent, which is the forty-day period of abstention from any excesses.

Lent begins with Ash Wednesday. It is a period of penitence which marks the forty day fast of Jesus in the desert. Sundays are excluded from this period, which culminates in the Festival of Easter. The final Sunday of Lent is called Mothering Sunday and traditionally *Simnel cakes* were baked then ready for Easter Sunday.

Holy Week is the seven days leading up to Easter, and Hot Cross buns symbolically depict the events of Good Friday and are eaten on this day. Easter Sunday marks the end of Lent with its associated austerities, and the start of rejoicing is reflected in a diet which may include Easter cakes and chocolate eggs. At Easter time the Orthodox Church will stain eggs a blood-like colour in memory of Jesus' death. Other churches may well decorate hard-boiled eggs.

In the Autumn the Christian churches celebrate Harvest. For many this is an act of giving to others rather than eating special foods. However it is common to share food together in various ways.

Christmas time celebrates the birth of Jesus and has traditionally been marked by the giving and receiving of presents. Special foods at Christmas include Christmas cakes and Christmas puddings as well as mince pies and turkey. As the UK becomes increasingly multi-cultural so too the Christian practices will begin to vary. For example some Eastern European countries eat fish, such as carp, rather than turkey. This will begin to affect some of the traditions within Christian practices in the UK.

There are other food customs which are associated very often with a localised part of the UK.

Hinduism and diet

There are many dietary variations amongst Hindus, so it is important not to oversimplify the situation. Variations occur from region to region as well because the extent of religious observance varies. It is stated in the laws of Manu:

> No sin is attached to eating flesh or drinking wine, or gratifying the sexual urge, for these are the natural propensities of man; but abstinence from these bears greater fruits.

In principle most Hindus are vegetarian, though in India there are some castes which eat meat, yet others eating fish. The taking of life whether human or animal is felt to be morally wrong. Life itself is of such importance to Hindus that the principle of non-violence is reflected in a belief called *Ahimsa*. To kill will effect a bad *Karma* which adversely effects future rebirths. Generally vegetarianism for the Hindu means not eating meat, fish or anything derived from them.

On a positive note, the cow is deemed a symbol of good maternal qualities such as unselfish love and gentleness. The five products from a cow are considered as purifying agents. These are milk, butter, curd, urine and dung. The eating of pork is banned as it is a scavenging animal. Those Hindus who are not strict may eat white fish or this may be a local custom. For example in Calcutta very many Hindus will eat fish.

In the UK outside of the home few Hindus are totally vegetarian, although beef is avoided by most. The fast-food establishments have wreaked havoc in this respect. The mother in the home will be more likely to observe vegetarianism because she will be the one who will perform *puja* or act of devotion before the shrine in the home. This will involve her being seated before the shrine with her head covered. Food and water are offered to the diety, with the uncooked food on the left and the cooked food on the right. Only after these devotions will the family sit and eat.

The issue of ritual cleanliness of food is of importance. As a principle it is reckoned that uncooked food is far less prone to contamination than cooked food. When food is cooked the 'qualities' of the cook are transmitted to the eater. It is possible to extend this argument by stating that to a certain extent the recipient partakes of the nature of the giver. This is reflected in the three main categories of food recognised by Hindus. Many families will seek a balance or equilibrium in their dietary patterns which reflects these categories:

> *Rajasic* (or demonic). Within this category are all meats as well as certain borderline foods such as mushrooms and onions. Chilli is said to stimulate excitement and action. Rajasic foods would never be recognised nor served in the Hindu Temple.
> *Sadvic* or *Sathvic*. These are peaceful foods associated with the gods. They promote harmony, intelligence and elevate the human spirit. Sathvic foods are considered the spiritual foods. These include, for example, all vegetables except mushroom and onions, milk products, sugar, rice, and fruit. They are deemed to keep the body 'light' as well as keeping the faculties clear.
> *Thamasic*. These are 'dull' foods, that is those which make you sleepy. Within this category are slightly stale foods such as previously cooked rice. These foods render the body heavy and cloud the faculties.

It is objectionable if permitted foods are mixed or physically come into contact with non-permitted foods. The result would be contamination. For most Hindus, dietary requirements are linked to their beliefs, yet it is difficult to generalise about the mixing or touching of foods. Within one family there may be differing beliefs and practices. It would not be unusual for a mother to be vegetarian and the father and children non-vegetarian. The spiritual person will seek to observe not mixing foods especially on auspicious days of fasting. Separate spoons would be used for separate dishes.

Fasting is also practised. This may be on an auspicious day such as Mahashivratri, or it may be linked to certain days of the lunar calendar or it may be linked to certain deities and temples. Many fasts will last 14 days but not necessarily so. The fast at Murgha (in November or December) is a very rigorous six day fast. Whilst fasting may involve abstention from all foods, for many it will involve abstention from certain types of food, for example, all those foods not considered pure. Fasting is undertaken for spiritual as well as physical purification, so there are various levels at which it will be practised. Some Hindus for example will take only one meal a day, whilst others may abstain totally for the six days, only taking a half a glass of milk daily at the temple. Others may well visit the temple each evening and eat fruit. After the fast the family will have Sathvic food which will have been prepared with new utensils such as pots, pans and spoons. The end of the fast will be marked by a small celebration.

In practical terms the parents may well fast but not the children unless they are at an age when they can choose to do so. Mr. Ratnasingham at the Ghanapathy Temple in Wimbledon describes it thus:

> Parents give their children an example to follow. It is rather like being given a route, the children deciding whether they wish to follow it. The example is set with the desire that the children will grow up recognising the existing system and adjust accordingly.

Both alcohol and tobacco are traditionally avoided by Hindus, but nowadays many males do use both in moderation and increasingly some women do so too.

There are associated foods linked to some Hindu festivals, though the variations locally are enormous. Holi, which is a Spring festival symbolising new life, uses the symbol of a coconut which is deemed a complete or perfect food because it contains milk, carbohydrate and protein. It is eaten as a symbol of good luck, which is taken to infer 'may your life be like the coconut which is complete'. Diwali, the Autumn festival of light symbolising the triumph of good over evil, of light dispelling darkness, is characterised by special sweet foods as well as sweets. Fasting precedes the feasting so care is taken in the preparation of the foods.

There are dozens of variants in terms of which festivals may be celebrated and whereabouts this takes place. The effect on schools within the UK is that the appropriateness of a festival for inclusion in a curricular activity may well depend on which Hindu community is represented within the local school community. The reader is recommended to consult books on Hinduism or to enter into dialogue with their local Hindu community to gain further details of foods associated with particular festivals.

Islam and diet

Fundamental to the Muslim attitude to food is the belief that it comes directly from God. This is reflected in two practical ways. Firstly there is always a sense of gratitude. Food is often not eaten until the Bismillah, the equivalent of a prayer of thanks, has been said either aloud or quietly. Meals are commenced and concluded with praise and gratitude to Allah. The second factor affects the attitudes towards excess. The Prophet Muhammad (pbuh) described Muslims as those who do not eat unless they are hungry, and that when they eat they do not fill themselves. It is recorded in the *Hadith*:

> No man fills a vessel worse than his stomach. A few mouthfuls that would suffice to keep his back upright are enough for a man, but if he must eat more, then he would fill one third with food, one third with drink and leave one third for easy breathing.

There is sufficient emphasis within the teachings of the Prophet for Muslims to adopt a disciplined style of practice in relation to food.

A key emphasis of Islam is for the individual to act responsibly before God and this includes how food is treated. Wasting food is seen as sin. Giving it to others or to animals is seen as preferable to throwing it away.

Islam has very clear instructions in relation to food. That which is not expressly prohibited is permissable. The Qur'an prohibits the following categories:

- that which intoxicates or interferes with the clear functioning of the mind;

- pork or any of its by-products;
- flesh of any animals not killed in the prescribed manner;
- blood;
- any food offered to a deity or being other than God.

These foods fall into the category of *Haram*, that which is forbidden. A devout Muslim would never partake of these knowingly. The category of foods which Muslims may eat is called *halal*. This category does not simply include meats killed in a particular manner, rather it includes vegetables and any foods which are clean, nourishing and healthy to eat. Between the categories of haram and halal is a category of foods called makrah. Food in this category is not recommended but would not be expressly forbidden. Examples are certain birds such as pigeon, eagle, seagull (this is regardless of the legal position in the UK relating to the latter two of these species).

Devout Muslims are those who practice the *Five Pillars* (see Chapter 7). These are deemed to give peace and freedom to the adherent because they reflect the position of a person at one with the expressed will of Allah. One of the pillars, observing Ramadhan, has a direct bearing on attitudes to food and self-denial.

Fasting is observed during the month of *Ramadhan*. During the daylight hours of this lunar month Muslims will abstain from all solid foods as well as liquids. Indeed the swallowing of one's spittle is not encouraged. Teachers need to be aware of this, when normal etiquette would discourage spitting. For the Muslim it is an act of obedience to Allah. During Ramadhan, Muslims will eat only after dark or early in the morning prior to sunrise. This will not be a problem for children in the primary school as observing the full fast is a matter of choice until adulthood has been reached. The younger child may practice missing a meal at weekends as part of the family training, but it is most unlikely to be an issue to cause worries at school.

The festival of *Id ul Fitr* marks the end of Ramadhan. Congregational worship is usual as a sign of joy and happiness. Muslim countries will observe this as a national holiday, and it is to be expected that Muslim children in this country will not attend school when the day falls within term time, especially as prayers and worship at the Mosque are viewed as of great importance on this festive occasion.

Another of the Five Pillars of Islam is that of *Zakat*, whereby a Muslim is required to give 2.5 per cent of their income to people less fortunate than themselves. At Id ul Fitr there is a special gift in almsgiving. This may be in the form of food. The value of the gift is reckoned to be the cost of a meal for the whole family. Foods associated with Id include samosas, carrot pudding, salad with yoghurt and sweets. After the self-discipline of the month of Ramadhan Id ul Fitr is a day of great rejoicing, feasting and happiness.

At the feast of *Id ul Adha*, which marks the hajj or pilgrimage to Makkah, another pillar of Islam, a cow or sheep will be killed, cooked and shared with no wastage. Friends, neighbours and the poor will share together on this occasion.

Judaism and diet

Jewish dietary laws have been established for 2,000 years. Inevitably this means that traditions are well established wherever the Jewish community is to be found. Food and diet for the Jew reflect well-established laws which specify which foods are permissible and which are not allowed. Jewish 'food' is inextricably bound to the Jewish Faith itself. It would be true to state that these dietary laws have brought a sense of unity, almost identity, to the home and the broader Jewish community. It is as if the very act or requirement to eat has become part of a unifying experience which has helped enable the Jewish identity to be maintained.

The *Torah* outlines the various food laws (in the books of Leviticus and Deuteronomy) which are strictly adhered to by the Orthodox Jew as well as being of fundamental importance to those from the Liberal and Reform traditions. In brief these may be summarised as follows:

- meat which has not been killed in the prescribed manner is forbidden;
- meat may only be eaten if the animal 'chews the cud and divides the hoof';
- fish is only to be eaten if it has both fins and scales;
- after eating meat no milk or milk products are permissible.

The general term covering Jewish dietary laws is *Kashrut* which means 'permitted'. *Kosher*, derived from the former term, has three dimensions. It means 'fit to be eaten'; it covers those foods which are permitted by dietary laws to be eaten and those categories which are forbidden (these are referred to within the Torah in Leviticus chapter 11 verses 1–43); finally it includes the separation of meat and milk. Meat and milk are neither cooked together nor eaten together. Jewish kitchens will therefore be divided into two distinct sections – one for meats and one for milk, with separate utensils for each. This separation encourages many Jews to be vegetarian in practice, thus minimising the practical difficulties, of mixing certain foods. Vegetarianism is not a religious requirement, however.

For Jews, foodstuff and its production are closely linked to matters of faith. God is deemed to be the Creator, and this brings with it both privilege and responsibility to the Jew. This religious sensitivity should permeate the Jewish thinking and those not of the Faith need to be aware of this. The way in which this works in practice will be developed later in this section. The complexity and minutiae of dietary requirements is such that many Jews will seek advice from their Rabbi on the more obscure practical aspects.

Closely allied to the belief that God is creator is the emphasis that God's people must learn to live humbly and obediently before Him. This finds expression in the Torah. Eating patterns are immediately affected by the fourth commandment:

> Remember the sabbath day and keep it holy.
> Six days you shall labour and do all your work,
> but the seventh day is a sabbath of the Lord your God
> therefore the Lord blessed the sabbath and made it holy.
> (Exodus 20 v 8-12)

The *Shabbat*, or Jewish Sabbath, commences at dusk on a Friday evening and the weekly meal brings together family, food and beliefs in a manner which has strongly influenced past practice and continues to epitomise the heart of the Jewish Faith and identity. Prohibition of work, during the Sabbath does not involve absence of food; rather dietary requirements are carefully planned for so that work on the Sabbath is not involved in their preparation. For Jews, the careful buying and preparation of food is virtually a symbolic reminder of God's presence and their promise to serve Him.

The eve of Sabbath meal and the setting of the table is symbolic in itself of Judaism. The setting includes the candlesticks to be lit by the mother, the *Kiddush* wine goblet used in the prayer of sanctification of the shabbat, the two plaited loaves called challah covered by an embroidered cloth, as well as the salt and wine used as part of the kiddish ceremony when the shabbat commences. Cooking of food to be eaten on the Saturday may have been commenced prior to the Sabbath. Indeed there are many meals associated with the Sabbath that are slow-cooked, such as Cholent, a meat and vegetable casserole.

It is only to be expected that a prayer of thanks (grace) will be said before meals, usually audibly.

Foods associated especially with festivals which revolve around the calendar means that there is a year-round interest in special foods. In these instances some of the foods will have either seasonal or symbolic connotations. Three examples are given below but I could equally have chosen any other festival from the calendar.

Rosh Hashanah, the Jewish New Year, is associated with honey cakes called Lekach, as well as apples and carrots. When honey cake and sweet wine are served it is to symbolise that the recipient should have 'sweetness' or pleasantness in the forthcoming year.

Purim, or the Feast of Esther, is associated with Hamantaschen which are triangular pastries filled with poppy seeds and brown beans.

Pesach, or Passover, is an eight day Spring festival which celebrates the exodus from Egyptian slavery. The passover story, or *Haggadah*, is read on the first two nights and is interwoven with a *Seder* meal. All the foods are truly symbolic of those historic events which have subsequently moulded Jewish identity and thinking. The unleaven bread or matzoth, reflects the speedy departure of the Hebrew people from Egypt, that is, they did not have time to wait for the bread to rise. Details of the first Passover can be found in Exodus chapter 12.

Some of the festival foods are well worth cooking with children at school. On several occasions in the primary classroom I have been involved with making potato latkes at the time of Hannukah. For many younger children peeling onions and potatoes is for them a first time experience. The class enjoyment in sharing the results is worth the effort of setting up a small group activity, ensuring necessary safety factors have been taken into account.

Sikhs and diet

Truthful living is fundamental in Sikh thinking, allied to the fact that there is a requirement that a Sikh should speak sweetly as before the Lord. There is emphasis therefore on the obvious fact that the mouth is the organ for speech as well as the organ for eating and drinking. Foods and drink should not harm the body. The *Guru Granth Sahib* teaches the virtue of self-restraint. Within Sikhism there are five vices and five virtues. The requirement on the Sikh is for a 'golden mean' between the two extremes so that life is one of balance and awareness before the Lord.

Not all Sikhs are vegetarian, but for those Sikhs who have undergone the Amrit, or initiation, ceremony, there are clearly defined codes of conduct in relation to diet which encourage vegetarianism. Allied to the belief in re-incarnation is the concept that the soul can be found in living objects such as animals. Animals must not be killed because the Lord is within. Yet if it were necessary to safeguard the survival of the Sikh Faith, for example during war, a devout Sikh may well eat meat (though special prayers would be said; the same applies to medicines which may contain impure substances). The basic principle in relation to foods is found in the holy book, the Guru Granth Sahib, where it is stated, 'Do not eat those things you do not grow'. So vegetarianism is positively encouraged within the Sikh community and is almost always practised at the Gurdwara, or temple.

The design of every *Gurdwara* includes a kitchen or *Langar*. This is because communal eating is part of basic Sikh belief and practice. The first Guru, *Guru Nanak Dev Ji*, established the principle of eating together. Bear in mind that Sikhism grew out of and away from the Faiths of Hinduism and Islam. Guru Nanak Dev Ji established the principle that all men and women are equal before God, and he therefore rejected the caste system of the day. At the langar in the Gurdwara opposite ends of the social strata will sit together. On this occasion, wealth, colour, creed and gender do not matter since the focus is the community sitting together to share a meal. The meal will have been prepared by a family or group of families who take it in turn to do this. This service to the langar is called Sewa, that is, doing a service to others. Members of the community will often bring gifts of food that will form part of the langar.

Whilst many Sikhs are strictly vegetarian, some, particularly in the West are not. Pork is considered unclean and not eaten, likewise many Sikhs will refuse beef. The lure of the fast food establishments has meant that traditional prohibitions are being challenged. Whilst many Sikhs will now drink alcohol, those who are devout will not imbibe alcohol because smoking and drinking are considered not to help the individual to concentrate on living their life for God.

Guru Gobind Singh Dev Ji the tenth Guru went hunting during his lifetime. He had other warriors with him called Nihansinghs who were always ready to fight to defend their Faith. At the time these warriors lived in the jungle and emerged at times of need. They were allowed to eat meat but they only killed that which was required for them to eat and survive, not for sport. Today these 'hidden' warriors now live in villages in India, and they are not vegetarian either at home or at the Gurdwara. There are currently no Nihansinghs residing in Britain, although they may be seen on horseback in the Punjab wearing their distinctive dark-blue garments and carrying an array of steel weapons.

The issue of not mixing foods or utensils does not apply at the Gurdwara as generally all Gurdwaras are vegetarian in practice. At home where individuals within the family may be at different stages of religious development, it is possible for individuals within families not to be vegetarian. In this context utensils will be kept apart. Meat utensils will not be used for the vegetarian dishes and vice versa. At school level the extent to which this is an issue will depend on the individual families.

Westernising influences on the home are varied in extent and are therefore relative. Sikh parents have the responsibility and duty to care for their children. This will include, when the children are older, parents discussing and sharing the reasons behind any instructions given. The role of the parents among Sikhs should never be underestimated. It is one of example. Certainly those parents who have undergone the Amrit ceremony would set a firm example for their children to follow. In teaching the child the tenets of the Faith, foundations are being laid which safeguard them for their future Faith development.

Part of Sikh practice is to use the Kirpan to acknowledge that food is *bhog*, or from the Lord. The kirpan, part of the 5 K's worn by Sikhs, is drawn across foods whether in the home or Gurdwara as a reminder that food is a gift from the Lord.

Implications for teachers

It is suggested that the following general principles are applicable for the teacher in school if religious dietary problems arise:

- Find out what is the child's normal diet. Use your existing knowledge of any religious requirements as a basis for conversation thus showing that you are trying to understand and the result should be the basis for the development of mutual understanding and trust. A child should not be forced to break a family religious requirement. Children often, for a variety of

motives, will wish to hide from a personal conflict and make a variety of excuses to hide the actual difficulty.
- If meals are cooked on the premises it is advisable to include those responsible for school meals in any discussions of this nature so that there will not be a clash between belief and practice. The school meals service may well be more aware than the school, and shared discussion would be helpful at this stage.
- Many fears exist amongst families that their dietary requirements will be ridiculed by those from outside the 'Faith'. It is entirely understandable that families should wish to follow their religious beliefs and practices and to compromise these in any way. It is not for the school to question this right, but as far as is practicable to accommodate pupils from a variety of religious backgrounds. For some this will mean eating typical 'British' foods, for others it will mean a restriction, or variation, of normal school practice.
- Schools should not presume that it is the mother or father who decide about dietary requirements. There may be occasion when it is appropriate to find and talk with the key personnel from the Faith. Without their support the school is vulnerable to external criticism. Increasingly Faith communities are joining in on discussions relating to their own Faith and its requirements for adherents.
- Teachers should be aware of the various dimensions of dietary requirements which may have implications on any cooking or work with food in the classroom itself.
- Most religious festivals will have links with special foods for the special occasions, and this needs considering when a multi-Faith approach is adopted in school.

CHAPTER 4

Appearance and Clothing Linked to Religion

Most religions have dress of particular types associated with them. These clothes are often worn by religious leaders as a sign of their role in relation to their Faith-community. Religion, for some, may involve the shaving of the head, whilst for others the hair will remain uncut. Some will mark their bodies in some way as a sign of devotion whilst others will deliberately refrain from publicising their beliefs through their appearance and clothing. Generally it is foolish to stereotype. It is possible however to write in general terms, especially if the practice is derived from the principles embodied within the holy writings, as is the case, for example, within Islam or Sikhism.

Buddhism

Whilst lay-Buddhists do not wear distinctive clothing, except on special occasions, the monks always do so. Part of the initiation rite as a monk includes the shaving of the head after travelling in style to the ceremony. This is symbolic of *Gautama* the Buddha laying aside his earthly possessions in his quest for truth. In Thailand for example, when a boy is about seven or eight years old he may become a novice monk. He will undergo an initiation ceremony and then live either at a temple or monastery with a mentor who will teach him the *Ten Precepts*. The boy will have his head shaved and he will wear the saffron robes associated with Buddhism. In Thailand the training will continue until the person has the choice of becoming a fully-fledged monk at the age of twenty. Of course very many do not continue as novices after a few months when young. Usually they become part of the active lay-community.

This practice of initiating novice monks is still unusual in the UK, but in the school Summer holidays of 1991 the Buddhapadipa Temple in Wimbledon admitted a group of eleven boys as novices. This was the first time this has occurred in the UK. This could only take place during the long Summer vacation and the boys were required by the monks to return to school in September. The length of time each boy attended varied from two weeks to one month. If the boys had been over the age of sixteen (or post-school leaving age) then they could have stayed on for longer. This period of time is called The Summer Ordination, during which the boys are taught to get up at 5 a.m., learn chanting, spend 30 minutes in meditation and at 7.30 a.m. will have breakfast. They will also receive religious instruction.

There is no prescription for particular colours to be worn nor any special style of clothing. However women lay-Buddhists tend to wear white clothes especially on the four prayer days of each month. These days are called *Wan pra* and are linked to the lunar calendar. For the male lay-Buddhists they too may wear white clothing on these days.

Several years ago I attended the Buddhist New Year festival of Song Kran at the Buddhapadipa Temple. It was surprising to find the equivalent of a beauty contest taking place (with modest styles of dress). It seemed to me quite incongruous at the temple. Subsequent enquiries revealed that this is associated with the story of the Seven Daughters which is celebrated annually on April 13th.

The story itself belongs to pre-history. It is not Thai in origin and reflects the Hindu story of Brahma, the god who had seven daughters. In a contest of wisdom Brahma was defeated by a wise man, and the penalty for defeat was death by beheading. Brahma was killed. However, one of his daughters carried his head on a tray since, as the head was holy, it would have caused the earth to burn with fire had it touched the ground. Afterwards on April 13th each year one of the daughters would carry the head in this manner. The 'beauty-contest' at Song Kran is loosely based on this tale! This intertwining of culture and festival is common within most Faiths.

In general terms the lay-Buddhist in the UK will not be bound by hard and fast rules over the style of clothing worn. Perhaps the greatest influence on the child growing up will be the influence of the parents and the home background. Many Buddhists will adopt Western dress styles for most of the time, possibly wearing traditional styles on communal occasions at the temple.

Christianity

The lay-community of Christians today generally do not wear distinctive clothing. As with many religious groups there is an emphasis on modesty so that natural instincts may be channelled in an acceptable manner. Over the centuries, however, certain religious groups have worn a distinctive type of clothing that has become almost a uniform. The puritans of the sixteenth and seventeenth centuries, for instance, had a modest style of clothing that can be found portrayed as a trade mark on a certain brand of porridge oats! Some of the Puritans' requirements are still evident amongst certain believing communities, so bright colours tend not to be worn by some when attending Church, whilst a head covering for women is still encouraged in some churches.

The position is very different from those who hold office in the Church. Most priests or ministers will wear the clothing of office and these may reflect denominational differences. At times the colour of the clothing changes according to the seasons. The styles of garb may have been the norm many centuries ago but they have not substantially altered with time. Consequently a cleric in full garb may appear to children to be wearing a 'dress'. Yet this distinctive appearance, often complete with a 'dog-collar', is used as a positive means of identification. The colour worn may also signify the 'rank' attained within the Church hierarchy. These comments apply especially to the Anglican, Catholic and Orthodox traditions. For example, a cardinal in the Catholic Church may wear red robes, whilst a bishop in the Anglican Church wears purple to signify his office. Many *Nonconformist* denominations have local leaders who may well dispense with the distinctive clothing whilst retaining the title of pastor, minister or reverend.

There are often special clothes worn by lay-Christians if they are choristers, or involved in rites of passage such as a christening, baptism, confirmation or marriage. In everyday wear some people will wear special jewellery that depicts a Christian symbol such as a cross or crucifix, but this is by no means limited only to Christians. Mention should be made of those nuns who are married to God and wear a silver 'wedding' ring to signify their devotion to God. There are various Christian monastic groups who wear distinctive dress. This is outside the scope of this book but many church schools will have staff from these backgrounds who wear the special clothing of monks or nuns.

Hinduism

The key to an understanding of Hindu attitudes towards dress is to accept the principle of modesty. Exposure, especially amongst women, is to be cautioned against thereby avoiding embarrassment and distress amongst conservative Hindus. Modesty will be applied to the whole body and therefore the wearing of clothes that cover the legs in public will usually be observed. This is standard practice amongst Hindu women and older girls and is now recognised by many British schools in their uniform regulations.

Mr. Ratnasingham at the Ghanapathy Temple in Wimbledon commented that the principle of modesty in dress originates from the temple where it is insisted upon as a priority. The role of the temple is to enable the individual to meet with god. Nothing should be allowed to distract from this and that includes appearance and behaviour. As the temple has a strong and dynamic influence on the home, parental roles at home and the examples set there encourage this principle to permeate life itself.

The Westernising influences are not a worry to many leaders of the Hindu community. Hinduism is a religion that is experienced and it tends to be adaptable to local circumstances rather than dogmatic, with the individual experiencing the religion for him/herself. As the foundations of the community and its Faith are strong, the fear of 'corrupting influences' is lessened. So long as the Temple has the central place, the individual can easily identify with the community which 25 years ago was very concerned about its identity. Some second-generation Hindus choose to wear saris, others adopt Western dress with very many choosing both styles depending on the occasion.

Many Hindu men wear dhotis, a long, loose fitting garment of about five to six metres in length. This is wrapped around the waist and drawn between the legs. Women may well wear a sari over a blouse and underskirt. The sari is a length of material also about five to six metres in length wrapped round the body. The midriff may sometimes be left bare. Hindu women of Northern Indian and Punjabi extract may wear the shalwar and kameez. The kameez is rather like a long shirt or tunic with half or long sleeves. The shalwar are baggy trousers. These may reflect trends in fashion and the lengths and style may vary. With these two items a woman would wear a long scarf called a chuni or dupatta which covers the head and breasts. As a sign of respect to strangers the head may also be covered.

Within Hinduism there is the Sacred Thread Festival called *Upanayana*. This can take place between the ages of 7–24 years for those boys of the *Brahmin* Caste. It is sometimes known as the second birth because in the first birth the Brahmin child comes from his mother, whilst the second birth is when he begins to learn from his guru, whose task it will be to teach him about religion. The thread worn by the boy, from this festival onwards, will have strands of white, red and yellow. The spiritual knot is called the Brahma Granthi. The thread symbolises the trinity. The strands remind him to control his mind, speech and body. The priest will whisper the *Gayatri Mantra* in his ear.

> Let us meditate on the excellent splendour of the sun-god Savitri; may he rouse our insights. (Rig Veda 3, 62, 10)

The sacred thread is worn both day and night. It is exchanged if it becomes dirty, and renewed at Hindu New Year. If there is a Brahmin boy in your class it is to be expected that the thread will be worn constantly and therefore should not be removed without discussion with the parents, if at all.

In the past the Brahmin boy would have left home and lived with and learnt from his guru. In this way the minds of the Brahmins were trained. Westernising influences in India have meant change. Many Brahmins progressed academically in the English schools and then chose careers outside of the priesthood especially in Civil Service administration in what was formerly British India.

However unchanged today is the fact that the Brahmin has a trained mind. With a population explosion in the Indian sub-continent, it is common now for the boy to remain at home but occasionally this 'leaving home' is symbolically re-enacted by the family. The boy may go round all his family and say 'goodbye', he may then 'beg' food from his mother and then set off with a staff in one hand and a begging bowl in the other, on a imaginary journey to his guru. He will leave home yet return almost immediately. The person adopting the role of the guru will always be another Brahmin, a *pandit* well versed in the Hindu scriptures. The guru will always be attached to the temple, though he may not necessarily be performing there daily as a priest.

When praying a Tilak mark will be placed on the forehead. This may be a red paste. The marks vary in design. Sometimes the marks designate which gods are worshipped. For example, three vertical lines show the devotee worships the deity Vishnu, while those with three horizontal lines are devotees of Shiva. Markings in red are called kumkuman (in Northern India, senthur) and depict happiness. Where holy ash is used in the temple, either as a line or a dot, this is a mark of humility. Holy ash may be used anywhere on the body. Its association with cremation acts as a reminder of purpose to the worshipper which is to seek peace and humility. However those markings used at weddings, such as painting of hands and feet, are purely cosmetic.

Hindus on occasions may wear jewellery or medallions depicting the wearer's own personal deity, or an amulet which may have been chosen and blessed by the priest or guru. At a wedding ceremony a necklace is given to the bride. The eternal name *Om* may often be worn as a badge or necklace. Some might see it as a talisman, others might well wear a thread on the wrist. These are usually removed at bedtime. Of great rarity in the UK will be the person who wears the thread with a small cylinder. This would be worn tightly around the neck and not removed. Likewise the Brahmin boy would never remove his sacred thread nor be expected to do so. If these are evident in school, then a discussion with the family should alleviate anxieties, spoken or unspoken, about their removal for certain school-based activities.

Islam

Islam encourages simplicity and modesty. Principles and limitations about Muslim dress are derived from the Qur'an and expanded further in the *Hadith* (the sayings of the Prophet *Muhammad* (pbuh)). It is usual for Muslims to wear clothes that may either reflect their country of origin or where they are now living. The fact that there are literally dozens of different styles of national dress which conform to the principles of Islam reflects how Islamic principles may work in practice.

Men keep themselves covered from the navel to the knees. The choice of wearing a head covering for prayers rests with the individual, though it is traditional for men and women to do so. Although women can wear clothes containing silver or gold, the same is not true for men for whom it is not allowed. Many Muslim women will only wear jewellery in the presence of their husbands. It is also preferred for unmarried girls neither to wear jewellery nor make-up. The over-riding principle expressed in practice is 'do not be provocative' in your style of clothing; there is also the principle that clothes designed for one sex may not be worn by the other.

Those who have completed the pilgrimage (the *Hajj*) to Makkah are called *Hajji*. They can now wear two white sheets of seamless cloth called ihram as a sign of equality before god. New or specially cleaned clothes are often worn at the end of *Ramadhan* and are particularly associated with the Festival of *Id ul Fitr*.

Of particular relevance to schools is the issue of *hijab* or purdah, whereby older girls or teenagers cover the whole of their body with loose fitting clothes as well as the face. Muslim women are expected to dress modestly and wear hijab (covering cloak) when going out or meeting adult males who are not close relatives. This does not mean that women must all wear one type of dress, though whatever is worn should clearly reflect the wearer's Islamic identity. Western society with its media pressures challenges these principles at a practical level, and children and young people in the UK may observe hijab to a greater or lesser extent. Many older female pupils may have conflicts with their parents' attitudes allied to Westernising influences when their peer group will be wearing skirts and modern styles of dress. It is the cause of many Muslim children leaving home at the first opportunity when they are old enough. This is a sensitive issue, one that is distressing to many parents as well as one that needs sensitive handling at school level. Some schools have variously adapted school uniform requirements so as to be sensitive to Muslim and Asian pupils and some LEAs have issued general guidelines in support of their schools. Within many LEAs it is now common for older female Muslim pupils to wear trousers to school thereby permitting hijab.

Judaism

The principle of modesty of dress may be found within the Jewish tradition. That which distracts from putting God first is discouraged. This may be extended to clothing and the human form. For everything there is a place but not if it conflicts with scriptural principles as embodied within the Torah.

Whilst the Orthodox tradition has very rigid guidelines, these generally will not affect the state sector of education for the orthodox community will have its own schools, thus preserving its traditions and beliefs. The reform or liberal branches of Judaism will distinguish between that which is acceptable within the synagogue and outside. So, for example, the reform tradition might well allow miniskirts at a party but feel that they are inappropriate within the synagogue because the nature and purpose of the place is very specifically directed towards the things of God. The attitude of the liberal/reform tradition is that these styles of dress are permissible to those outside of the Faith and to the Jew outside of the synagogue, but not desirable within the synagogue itself.

The majority of orthodox male Jews will keep their heads covered during waking hours. This would include children. The Hassidim do not cut the corners of their hair, consequently the ringlets are prominent below the ears. Traditionally Orthodox Jewish women will wear a wig to hide their hair from those not within the family. They may wear a head covering whilst at the synagogue and also when performing the Shabbat prayers at home.

Most male Jews will wear a headcovering when they are praying or studying the scriptures. The name given to the small skull-cap worn is kapel or Yamelkah. This would always be worn at prayer times in addition to the prayer shawl called a tallith. The tallith is a four cornered shawl with tassels at each corner. This dates from a reference within the Torah (Numbers 15 verses 37-41) which refers to the fringes of the garments. Deuteronomy 22 verse 12 mentions the four corners of the covering. The Tallith may well be the only four-cornered garment still worn and the tzitzit or fringes on the shawl remind the wearer of the Torah and the Unity of God. Other items worn when praying are the Tefillin. These consist of two leather boxes worn on the left arm and head. The boxes contain four passages from the Torah (Exodus chapter 13 verses 1-10, 11-16; Deuteronomy chapter 6 verses 4-9 and chapter 11 verses 13-21). Prayer is a time of total and absolute concentration on God and these items assist in this task.

Mention should be made of the Kittel which is a long white robe worn as a sign of humility. It may be worn by the head of the house at the Passover seder, or used as a burial shroud. It may also be worn in the synagogue at Yom Kippur, though this is increasingly rare, and may or may not be linked to the following example of being humble told to me by David Clarke.

A rabbinic story of Yom Kippur relates how a rabbi threw himself on the ground in abject humility exclaiming, 'I am but dust and ashes!' This was rapidly followed by the cantor adopting the same procedure. Not wishing to be outdone the caretaker was seen to throw himself on the floor in humility loudly proclaiming, 'I am but dust and ashes!' The rabbi could be overheard commenting to the cantor, 'Now look who thinks he's dust and ashes!'

Sikhism

In the UK today there is a mix of traditional and Western clothing. Most women wear Shalwar and Kameez for comfort both in terms of modesty and culture. This is especially true at the Gurdwara. Younger children growing up in the UK are increasingly influenced by Western styles and fashions. Styles of dress at the Gurdwara also vary significantly amongst the men. For both men and women their age very often determines their preferred style of dress.

Practising Sikhs of both sexes will always observe the wearing of the 5 K's of their religion. They are called the 5 K's because each item worn begins with the letter 'K' in Punjabi. All initiates will wear the 5 K's proudly and it would compromise their Faith if any of them were not worn. The extent to which non-initiates wear these items will vary greatly, according to context and environment. The extent to which younger children wear all the 5 K's also seems to vary in the UK.

Kesh, the first of the 5 K's, is the term used for the uncut hair. This is a symbol of devotion to God. Most Sikhs will never have their hair cut, certainly after they have been initiated, though some adult Sikhs who have not been initiated may cut their hair. Western fashion trends have meant that some males may trim their beards or have shorter hair and not wear a turban, whilst some ladies may trim the length of their hair. This means that in practice variations will occur amongst children. There are those who will not have their hair cut at any stage in their childhood. Their parents will be nurturing them in the Faith and encouraging the self-discipline required of a committed Sikh. Western influences in terms of styles and fashions have now reached the cities of India as well as determining practice amongst the younger people within the UK.

The fact that the hair symbolises devotion to God means that it will always be cared for. The turban is worn to keep the hair tidy as well as being a public declaration that the person is a Sikh. A devout fifteen year old boy, Amarjit Singh, told me 'It is my religious duty to look after my hair, it is part of my daily prayers'. The hair will be washed regularly, and for many this will be daily. In the Gurdwara the head is always covered, regardless of the length of hair. If a teacher were taking a group of children to the Gurdwara then a head covering should be worn by the visitors as well as removing the shoes prior to entering the prayer hall of the Gurdwara. Whilst the majority of men wear the turban, the women wear a scarf called a dupatta. These can vary in style, colour and length according to personal preference.

The *patka*, a headcovering which holds the shape of the head with room for the hair to be worn as a 'jura' or 'top knot', may on occasions be worn by children in the UK for activities such as swimming. Far more common is for children, under the age of about 10, to wear the hair in plaits. Wearing the plaits helps the hair to grow in length. It also allays a sense of anxiety or apprehension with their school peer group as it is much closer to Western styles. Some Sikhs at this point will wish to be excused from certain school activities such as swimming so that they do not draw attention to themselves. A child wearing the turban, having to remove it for swimming, may make himself an object of attention from others. The teacher should exercise great sensitivity and awareness of how vulnerable children are at certain stages in their lives. One young Sikh interviewed about this matter said that if he had had the courage to remove the turban once without adverse comments from the others at school swimming classes then he might have done so regularly. However his apprehension was such that he did not wear the turban at school and continued swimming. Another Sikh said that he had requested his parents to write a letter excusing him from swimming rather than remove the turban. These examples show opposite courses of action but do not really reveal the personal anguish felt by both young people.

The wearing of the turban will commence when the parents feel the child is able to cope with the outside world and can handle the responsibilities which will arise with the public declaration of their identity. In the UK the age at which this will occur may well be at puberty. In India and the Punjab it would probably be at a younger age. This first wearing of the turban will be a significant occasion within the life of the family as well as the individual. It is usually marked with a family party, maybe even celebrated at the Gurdwara. The child will be given gifts to mark the occasion. There is no equivalent ritual for girls.

There are a variety of headcoverings worn by the male children as they grow up. Very common in India is the Patka as described above. The Patka comes in two sizes. The large size would be worn instead of a turban, the smaller size would be worn under the turban in case the turban came off.

The *Kanga* or the comb is the second of the 5 K's. The comb is a sign of discipline. Whilst it is always worn after initiation, in the West it is not always worn by young Sikhs. The purpose and uses of the comb vary. It has a practical function when it is used as a comb to care for the hair each day. Additionally it is used to keep the hair in place on the top of the head after the jura has been made. It is also a sign that the person is following Sikh traditions which require devotees to wear the 5 K's.

The third 'K' is the *Kachha* (or Kashaira) which is the baggy underwear. This is a symbol of freedom from the religious rules of Hinduism. Initially they were worn as a rejection of Hindu dhotis, but also as underclothes at a time when this was not common. The size of them reflects the period of the time when Westerners were wearing breeches and long-johns. In that context they are not unusual in size. Teachers should not bring undue attention to the Kachha. Very many young Sikhs will not wear the Kachha though it has to be stated that the recent trend towards boxer-shorts style underwear in the UK has alleviated many anxieties felt by Sikhs. An initiate will never totally remove this religious symbol.

A discussion with parents would help when it comes to PE/apparatus or games if there are any anxieties in this respect.

The fourth 'K' is the *Kara* which is a wrist bracelet. This bracelet is a symbol of strength as well as reflecting God's eternal nature and the unity of the Khalsa (the Brotherhood of Sikhs). It is a steel bracelet worn on either wrist. Sometimes the Kara is made out of gold, but spates of muggings have meant this is not so common as the stainless steel. It is usual for the Sikh child to receive the Kara at the initial naming ceremony in the Gurdwara. It is replaced with larger karas as the child grows towards adulthood.

The *Kirpan*, the fifth 'K', is a dagger or sword symbolic of the willingness of the believer to defend the Faith when necessary. Whilst the ceremonial sword may be up to a metre in length these would only be used at special occasions at the Gurdwara, such as Baisakhi, or be a symbolic decoration in the home. The majority of Sikh children within the UK will wear an ornamental or miniature kirpan which represents no challenge to either criminal law or school rules. Older Sikhs if wearing a kirpan would always have it out of sight whether in school or in the community. Amongst symbolic kirpans worn by children I have seen broaches or even badges. It is rarely an issue for a classteacher to be anxious about.

Implications for the teacher

There is an obvious possibility that school rules may clash with religious practices when it comes to appearance and clothing. Many schools will have a policy on such matters as uniform and jewellery. The school policy is usually based on the principles of security, equality, as well as those issues involving health and safety at work. The vast majority of parents will both recognise and respect this. It becomes obvious that there is the need for initial dialogue between school and home when children commence their schooling.

So many cultures have a positive attitude towards education and schooling, that with sensitive dialogue controversial issues can be obviated. Generally parents do not wish their child to be the odd one out but if confronted would dig in their heels on matters of religious principle. Interviewing staff need some form of training in these matters.

Some of the matters indicated in this chapter are of great symbolic significance because they are issues of personal, communal and religious identity. Children should never be the pawns in the debates. It may be necessary for a school to contact a local Faith community to ascertain the accuracy of claims being made by the child or parents, but again that may be handled sensitively in a manner that links positively the religious and school communities.

Some schools have variously adapted school uniform requirements so as to be sensitive to Muslim and Asian pupils. Some LEAs have issued general guidelines in support of their schools.

It may also be helpful to add that aspects affecting health and safety at work are areas that variously affect religious groups. This may be another source of information for the school in seeking guidance in controversial matters.

In short, the foremost principles for teachers have to be:

> do not stereotype,
> do not presume,
> do your homework and
> maintain dialogue in a positive and sensitive manner.

CHAPTER 5

Language, Sacred Writings and Religion

Prior to its demise, the Inner London Education Authority conducted a biennial census of pupils within its schools catchment area of those who used a language other than English at home. The most recent census recorded in 1989 showed that 70,221 pupils in London schools used a language other than English at home. A total of 184 languages were recorded. There are thus many children for whom English is a second or even a third language. Most cultures for whom there is a language of religion will seek to safeguard its position with special provision, either through the LEA, the home or the local place of worship.

It is almost a truism to state that some languages may be associated with certain religions, yet the point must be made. The languages associated with religion mean that the nature of language learning can serve a variety of functions. It will enhance a sense of communal identity and belonging. It will obviously be linked to religious knowledge and understanding as well as linking families closely across the world. This chapter is more concerned with language as it impinges on religion rather than simply on language *per se*. It also explores the language used in the sacred writings of that Faith as this may affect the children in school as that may be the language being taught or used at home.

The language of Buddhism

The ancient language of Buddhism is that of Pali. The majority of people able to read Pali are those who are Buddhist monks or scholars. The average lay-Buddhist would not be trained in Pali, though he or she may be in the language of the local Buddhist community. Buddhist communities within the UK, currently more than 100 in number, are spread throughout all parts of the country. They serve as a focal point for the understanding and development of the Buddhist Faith and its practices within the UK. Many of these centres will be responsible for the provision of particular language classes which will tie in with the community from which they originate as well as the community they serve.

For example the Buddhapadipa Temple, in Wimbledon which has the *sangha*, or monks, living on site, serves the Thai community and is its focal point. Lessons in Thai are given here each weekend together with meditation classes. Adults, as well as children, wishing to learn more of Buddhism and meditation practices will also attend these classes. The point being made here is that this type of provision has many purposes and is not narrowly orientated. For some it is clearly tied into Faith, for others it is cultural, or social or simply linguistic.

For most Buddhists the Temple is where the Sangha is to be found, and this is central to Buddhist philosophy and personal development. Whilst the monastery or Temple may well have a fairly elaborate shrine as a focal point for devotions most Buddhist families will also have a shrine in their home. It is usually on a smaller scale, similar rather than the same, and it may well have a separate or special room but not necessarily so. For those who cannot afford this space then regular visits to the temple will be made especially on the four prayer days each month. Increasingly it is quite usual for lay-Buddhists in the UK to observe the Sunday as their special day for observance of Buddhist practice.

The sacred scriptures of Buddhism, the *Tripitaka* (or Prah Tripidok in Thai) are written in Pali. The term Pali literally means 'scriptural text'. This distinguishes it from any commentary or interpretation of the text. Pali is the language of Theravada Buddhism, a fairly conservative form of Buddhism. Each full set of scriptures has forty-five volumes, so it is rarely found outside the Temple, monastery or in institutions of learning. The Tripitaka has been translated into Thai and English. (All three translations, including Pali, can be found at Buddhist centres such as the Buddhapadipa Temple in Wimbledon.) Because of its great length it is clearly impractical for the average lay-Buddhist to have a full set of scriptures at home. More commonly owned is the one-volume condensed version written in, for example, Thai. This adds an additional emphasis to the provision of Thai language classes within the lay 'Thai' community, though versions are also to be found in various other mother-tongue languages. As Buddhism is an international religion there are those who speak many indigenous languages.

The word Tripitaka literally translates as the Three Baskets. Originally written on palm leaves the sacred texts have three main sections.

- The Vinaya pitaka deals with the origins of Buddhism and disciplines of the life of a monk or nun.
- The Sutta pitaka deals with the nature of Buddhism and a doctrinal exposition of the teachings of the Buddha.
- The Abidhamma pitaka deals with the discipline of the mind.

The northern Buddhists, the Mahayana, accept the Tripitaka but have other books as well. These are the *sutras* (a term which literally means 'threads'), which are a collection of rules or sayings. There are a great many of these sutras.

Whilst Buddhism has no central credal statement, great emphasis is laid on *the Four Noble Truths* and *the Eightfold Path*.

In brief the Four Noble Truths are:

(1) that all life is suffering,
(2) that suffering derives from desire,
(3) cessation of suffering occurs when desire is extinguished,
(4) this can be achieved through the Noble Eightfold Path.

The Eightfold Path includes:

> Right Understanding
> Right Thought
> Right Speech
> Right Action
> Right Vocation
> Right Effort
> Right Mindfulness
> Right Concentration

The reader should find out more details from authentic Buddhist sources as to the exact meaning of these terms and how these are worked out in practice. Note carefully that the main emphasis for practice rests with the individual rather than looking to a deity outside of oneself.

The language of Christianity

Christianity has many millions of adherents from all over the world. The common practice within the Christian community has been to translate the Bible into as many languages and dialects as possible.

This has then been used as a tool for evangelism as well as encouraging growth in the Faith itself. Consequently there is very little demand made of the lay-Christian to learn the original languages of the sacred text. Many ministers or priests are not scholars in this sense.

At the end of 1991 the Bible Society stated that the number of complete translations of the whole Bible numbers 318. There are a further 726 languages into which the New Testament alone has been translated, with a further 902 languages into which a single book of the Bible has been translated. This means that there is a total of 1,946 languages into which at least one book of the Bible has been translated.

The Christian Bible has two main sections, the Old and the New Testaments. The Old Testament is composed of 39 books written originally in Hebrew. This section of the Bible is also regarded as authoritative by the Jews. With the advent of the Greek language in the second century BC, a Greek version of the Old Testament called the Septuagint emerged, though this included additional writings now known as the Apocrypha. The New Testament is composed of 27 books and was written in Greek. By the fifth century AD the whole Bible had been translated into the language of the Western Church which was Latin. The result of these complex developments has meant that today there is a far greater emphasis on having the scriptures in one's own language rather than learning the original languages of the sacred texts.

In relation to the classroom it is not really necessary to stress the nature of the language of Christianity simply because this is not done so by the majority of the Christian community. This is not to imply that Christianity does not have a specific terminology as part of its vocabulary. It does, and this should form a natural element within the Religious Education programme when dealing with Christianity.

The adage that 'familiarity breeds contempt' was brought home to me in the classroom when using a class set of Bibles. Having asked two twelve year olds to distribute them, they did so in the usual manner adopted by children when giving out books. That one fell off the desk was not perceived as 'wrong' or that they should not be handled and distributed normally. This attitude towards copies of the Bible was brought home to me by a Muslim pupil in the class who told me quite sincerely that her classmates should show a greater reverence for the Bible because it was the holy book of the Christians. Her sensitivity was evident and her hurt quite apparent. I learnt an important lesson from her that day which I will never forget.

Within Christianity there have been various important credal statements. Today the majority of Christians in the West would subscribe to what is often called the Apostles' Creed, although there are minor differences of interpretation of doctrine. The Eastern Church tends to adopt the Athanasian Creed. Acceptance of the creeds tended to be linked to initiation rites and was a sign that a person was ready to be a full church member together with its attendant responsibilities. The creeds tend to have three sections concerned with God, Jesus and the Holy Spirit. It is structurally based on St. Matthew chapter 28 verse 19.

The language of Hinduism

Most Hindus in Britain speak either Gujarati or Punjabi reflecting whence their families originated. If sending out letters in mother-tongue languages it is sensible to use the written form of Punjabi which is called Gurmurkhi. This written form of language unites speakers of several differing spoken languages. Hindi may be added to that list as another common Northern Indian language. Hindi is the language used in educational establishments, for example in Higher Education. Whilst there are literally hundreds of languages and dialects spoken in the Indian sub-continent, Hindi could be described as the majority language. Generally in Southern India, the Dravidian languages such as Tamil, Telegu and Kammabam are spoken.

The Community itself has taken seriously its responsibility for fostering and transmitting mother-tongue languages. Many communities in the UK will run language classes on a Saturday or Sunday, some being assisted by grants from their local authority. Whilst a few schools have started to teach these minority languages, many leaders in the communities feel that this is their duty and would not encourage this practice. The teaching of language is seen by the community as an important element in fostering and maintaining cultural identity.

Having evolved over 4–5000 years, Hinduism has no single book that may be referred to by all Hindus as the norm for belief and practice. The religion has been shaped by many varying thoughts and practices as well as many holy writings over many centuries, and it has no one central body to which it is possible to refer for a definitive statement about Hinduism, nor does it have a central credal statement. For Hindus believe that there are many ways in which followers may learn and live their Faith. The destination is the same, the route taken may vary. The result of this is that a simple definitive statement regarding Hinduism is either simplistic or inaccurate. Hinduism for the non-Hindu will therefore appear to be difficult to understand. Yet there is an underlying unity within Hinduism which establishes the religious principles to be followed by the individual. The main emphasis within Hindu diversity is for the individual to recognise that only part of truth and reality can be discerned. It is irrelevant to ask who is right and who is wrong. Stereotyping in relation to Hindus should thus be carefully avoided.

Amongst the vast body of Hindu sacred writings may be found two broad categories into which sacred writings may be placed.

The *Sruti* are those derived from the holy men, the rishis, and what was revealed to them by the gods. These truths are therefore eternal in nature. Literature in this category includes the *Vedas* and the *Upanishads*.

The *Smriti* are those truths handed down from generation to generation before finally being written down by wise men. Within this category of slightly lower order writings are the *Mahabharata*, the *Ramayana* and the *Laws of Manu*.

The elements of these writings which are commonly linked to classroom practice would be those usually linked to festivals. So, for example, the story of Rama and Sita may be found within the Ramayana and is popular when considering the festival of Diwali. Very many teachers use this story, often using drama as the medium against which children learn of the triumph of good over evil.

The language of Islam

The language of Islam is Arabic. It is believed by Muslims that the sacred text, the *Qur'an*, was orally transmitted to the Prophet *Muhammad* (pbuh)[1] by God's messenger, the Angel Gabriel (or, Jibra'il).

The sacred text is believed never to have been altered and the accuracy of it is maintained because the original language gives it this purity in transmission. Muslims will frequently attempt to learn Arabic as a way of transmitting the Faith to their children. Islam is a missionary Faith and these factors together with cultural issues of identity are all interwoven. Muslims believe that the Qur'an contains

Allah's guidance for humanity in its original language and form. The message of the Qur'an is valid for all times and conditions. As such it is a complete book of guidance and the text is jealously guarded. There may well be an inherent difficulty in using the Qur'an in the classroom. The education system of the UK is liberal-critical in basis and as such the study of sacred writings is an accepted part of any academic course in theology. However Muslims believe that such is the nature of the sacred Qur'an that it must never be subjected to such critical analysis. Many Muslims are prepared to make such analysis of the Bible which they would not allow for the Qur'an.

The language of Urdu has the same basic alphabet as Arabic, so for very many Asian Muslims Urdu is a language of great importance. Within the home reading and writing will be based on Urdu. Many parents will teach their children the Qur'an. The importance of the mother's role within Islam should be noted. The steady progression and development of the child in the parents' religion usually falls on the mother. Many will choose an appropriate time of day and assume the role of religious mentor by example and teaching. Many mothers will do this at a set time each day, such as in the morning when the child has been refreshed by sleep and is therefore more alert. Some families will engage a home tutor for their children to learn the basic teachings and rudiments of the Faith. This is, of course, in addition to any classes organised at the local mosque.

The term Qur'an means 'recite' or 'read'. The Angel Gabriel recited the words to the Prophet Muhammad (pbuh). The first revelations were in the year 610 CE. Within a short time of the death of the prophet all these revelations were brought together (650 CE). There are 114 suras or chapters in the Qur'an. The style of writing is that of poetry. Content varies from matters of doctrine, such as the Five Pillars, to more 'mundane' matters of law covering issues as diverse as, for example, inheritance, usury and business affairs.

The Qur'an is used as part of the prayers both at home and in the mosque. The writings are treated with the utmost respect. It is kept wrapped up when not in use. Symbolising that no other book may have a higher place it is kept in a high place above other books. Muslims will wash prior to reading it. Because it is handled as little as possible a special stool will be used. The name Hafiz will be given to anyone who has learnt the Qur'an by heart. Children will attend weekend or evening classes to learn Arabic and receive instruction in the meaning of the Qur'an.

Additional Holy writings for Muslims, though subordinate to the Qur'an, are as follows.

The *Hadith* literally means 'traditions'. It contains the words of the Prophet and his recorded wisdom in interpreting some of the principles contained in the Qur'an. Amongst the many practical matters included are details on hygiene, extravagance and manners.

The *Sunna*, contains the custom by which Islamic belief and conduct is regulated. Included are matters that neither the Qur'an nor the Hadith deal with. The Sunna has sought to determine the correct Muslim attitude.

A central credal statement in Islam is the Shahadah which is the first of the *Five Pillars of Islam*. This statement maintains,

> There is no God but Allah and Muhammad is His Messenger.

This summarises the essence of Islam as a whole and is sometimes referred to as the Kalimah. It is used in the five daily prayers and at various stages of life from birth through to death.

There are certain practices that would be observed by Muslims whether in the home or mosque. These would need to be safeguarded in the classroom. Amongst these would be the careful handling of the sacred scriptures. As explained above, the Qur'an at home would be kept on the highest shelf in the room. Within the classroom that practice may prove difficult to observe. Muslims will always wash their hands prior to handling the sacred text. Again this might be awkward for the teacher to observe whilst maintaining classroom control.

Generally a teacher would be unwise to have a copy of the Qur'an in the classroom if they could not guarantee this level of respect. I have found from experience that it is helpful when a Muslim child brings a copy of the Qur'an into school to keep it either in the staffroom or the Headteacher's room until it may be required in the classroom. I then ask the Muslim child to go and wash his or her hands and bring the sacred text into the classroom. I would not allow other children to handle it, but I would encourage them to look at the Arabic script and then ask the Muslim pupil whether he or she could read any of it. If he or she is able to read it in front of their friends the result is usually one of enhanced self-respect for the Muslim child and admiration from those within the class. This provokes excellent conversation and discussion as the children often have plenty of questions to ask each other. At a suitable point the child can then return the Qur'an to the staffroom to be collected at the end of the day.

The language of Judaism

The language of Judaism is Hebrew. It is one of the world's oldest extant languages. It has its own alphabet and it is the language of the scriptures, the *Torah*. The Orthodox community today use Hebrew in all their services, and symbolically Hebrew is treated as a vital link with the past as well as a unifying feature for contemporary international Jewry. The Orthodox community will allow a local language translation to be used in services for those who do not understand Hebrew, but only Hebrew will be used for public prayer. Progressive Jews within the UK, which includes the Liberal and Reform traditions, will use a combination of Hebrew and English.

Hebrew has been adapted over the centuries. So for example, the *Askenazi* use Yiddish which is a mixture of Hebrew and German. At one time, the *Sephardim* used a language called Ladino which is a mixture of Hebrew and medieval Spanish. Both Yiddish and Ladino are written with Hebrew letters, though the latter is rarely spoken today.

The Jewish scriptures are called the *Tenach*, called the Old Testament by Christians. Within the Tenach are the first five books called the Torah or the Five Books of Moses. The Torah is usually in scroll form and kept in the synagogue. Whilst the Tenach is important, the Torah is the fundamental basis of belief and practice. The first five books are therefore of great significance as well as being used in liturgy and festive occasions.

Torah scrolls are handwritten by scribes and are always treated with extreme veneration and respect. In the synagogue the Torah scroll is kept in the Holy *Ark*, above which the Eternal Light or Ner Tamid is burnt perpetually. The scrolls are written on vellum and are therefore never touched with the hand or fingers in case the natural oils of the skin blemish the skin of the scroll. A pointer or Yad, usually made from silver, is used to guide the eye.

Additional writings of importance are the rabbinic traditions called the *Talmud*. These date from 2,000 years ago. The Talmud contains legal codes as well as religious customs. The width of subjects is extensive, ranging from science, industrial relations and sexual problems.

The central statement of Faith is called the *Shema*. These are the

Biblical passages which affirm the unity of God and acceptance of His commandments. The passages concerned are Deuteronomy chapter 6 verses 4–9, chapter 11 verses 13–21 and Numbers chapter 15 verses 37–41. The Shema is used twice daily in liturgy as well as a night-time prayer.

The Jewish community lay great emphasis on the learning of Hebrew. This is one of the roles of the synagogue and language classes take place there on a regular basis, usually on the Sunday. Jewish children in the classroom will almost invariably attend these classes, and boys will be preparing for their *Bar Mitzvah* at the age of 13 whilst girls will be preparing for their *Bar Mitzvah* at the age of 12. Part of these ceremonies includes scripture reading in the Hebrew language.

The language of Sikhism

The sacred scriptures of Sikhism are called the *Adi Granth* or *Guru Granth Sahib*. This means 'First Collection' or 'Compilation'. Sahib means Lord and is added as a term of respect. Its basis lies in the poetic compositions of *Guru Nanak Dev Ji*, the founder of Sikhism and the Guru Granth Sahib includes 974 of his hymns. These scriptures were originally transmitted orally in Punjabi. The fifth Guru Arjan Dev Ji made an authoritative collection in 1604, which he installed at Harimandir. By 1708 the contributions of six Gurus had been included and the canon was closed and declared to be the Sikhs' Guru. The fact that this sacred text also included the work of twelve non-Sikhs reflects the open nature of the Sikh Faith. Early texts were hand written. The standard length of the sacred writings is 1430 pages.

The contents are similar to the book of psalms in the Judaeo/Christian Bible. It contains no narrative passages, but poems of praise and exhortations to hear the voice of God. Many hymns reflect an ethical and social concern. The opening words express the basic Sikh beliefs and are called the *Mool Mantra*. In English these are:

> God is only One.
> His Name is True.
> He is the Creator.
> He is without fear.
> He is inimical to none.
> He never dies.
> He is beyond births and deaths.

He is self illuminated.
He is realised by the kindness of the true Guru.
Repeat His Name.

The *Dasam Granth* forms part of a secondary collection of sacred writings. This contains the poetry of *Guru Gobind Singh Dev Ji*. It was compiled in 1734 and has 1428 pages.

The sacred writings are treated with the utmost respect. They are treated symbolically and in actuality as the living words of God, the Supreme Guru. So whether the writings are in the home or in the Gurdwara, similar standards of procedure are applied. In the home there needs to be a separate bedroom in which the Guru Granth Sahib may rest at night. The reader will always wash and perhaps have a bath prior to reading. The writings are always kept under a Rumalah or cover when not being read, and should never be in a smoke filled room. Sikhs will always bow or prostrate before the Guru Granth Sahib.

Only a few Sikhs will have their own copies of the complete scriptures because of this need for it to have a room on its own. Each morning the owner would have to rise before dawn, take a bath and read it. A similar pattern would be followed in the evening. The Guru Granth Sahib is definitely not an item to be kept on the shelf! It has a position of honour in the Gurdwara and is on a raised dais higher than the seated worshippers.

It is central to the various rites of passage such as naming or weddings. Prior to certain events it is read through in total, a process called the *Akhand Path*. Where a family do not have the complete scriptures at home, use will be made of the Sacred Nit Nem which is a daily prayer book containing a selection from the Guru Granth Sahib.

An additional practice within the Sikh community which reflects the importance of the scriptures for daily living is the equivalent of a verse for the day. This may be in written form pinned to a notice board at the Gurdwara. This is called a *Vak* or *Hukam*. Many Sikhs will now dial a special British Telecom number to hear this verse for the day which has been pre-recorded.

There are perhaps 60 million Punjabi speakers in the Indian subcontinent. Where Punjabi is in written form relating to holy utterances then the language is called Gurmurkhi, which literally means 'from the Guru's mouth'. In the UK, the local authority sometimes will sponsor Punjabi classes, but more commonly this is a function of the Gurdwara and serves to reinforce the culture and religion of the Sikh community.

Implications for teachers

Most children from religious minority groups will be learning a mother-tongue language which may well make English their second language especially when the mother-tongue language is the language of their religion. Children are then under enormous pressure to meet educational, religious and communal demands and teachers need to be sensitive to this.

As teachers we also need to be sensitive to the nature of the material we handle. There are dangers in studying that which is sacred without recognising in practical terms the way the Faith community itself handles its sacred texts.

In most instances use of the sacred text in the classroom should be limited or very carefully controlled. To develop the concept of the sacred amongst the children, a visit to a place of worship to see the sacred text may prove to be of greater educational value than running the risk of offending pupils of the Faith by bringing the text to the classroom.

Note

1. Occasionally in text books on Islam the reader will come across the abbreviations PBUH or pbuh. Always within Islam there is deference paid to the Prophet Muhammad and when his name is spoken the comment in Arabic is added which means 'Peace and Blessings Be Upon Him'. In books this is usually written (pbuh). Often in dialogue with Muslims the same deference is shown to the prophet Jesus.

CHAPTER 6
The Calendar and Religious Festivals

There are various calendars in use across the world. Where these are religious calendars they are usually tied in to a key event within that religion.

For many people, religious festivals and celebrations are linked to a lunar calendar. The obvious result of this is that festival dates will vary from year to year as the lunar year is 13 days less than the solar year. Some festive dates are fixed to a particular date in history and so are celebrated annually at a fixed date.

The school year in the UK reflects the underlying Christian history of this country, and the patterns of school holidays reflect the 'holy days' of Christianity. While the principal holy days of Christianity are thus 'safeguarded', this of course has practical implications for those of Faiths other than Christianity. However, when their holy days fall within term time, it does allow for immediacy and relevance in the teaching of multi-Faith RE, whereas Christian festivals tend to be celebrated during the holiday period.

There is an increasing tendency among authors of school textbooks to reflect the plurality of society and the more traditional BC/AD dating system is being rewritten as BCE/CE. This represents Before Christian Era/Christian Era.

Charts on religious festivals for each of the Faiths is included in this chapter. These are not exhaustive nor in some instances fully inclusive. They are designed to assist the classteacher to see at a glance the main details or characteristics of a particular festival. A section has been included which hints at the thematic element or the concepts which could be developed in the classroom.

The Buddhist calendar

The Buddhist year is based on the solar calendar, as in the West. 1991 CE is the same as 2534 BE (Buddhist Era) for those living in

Thailand. The dating system marks the year after the death of the Buddha. In some countries, such as Sri Lanka, the Buddhist calendar dates from the birth date of the Buddha, and so an additional 80 years will be added to the figure 2534 making 2614 BE. The majority of Buddhists, including those in the UK, celebrate from the year after the death of the Buddha, though historically there has been argument as to the precise year.

Contemporary Buddhists therefore live in what they refer to as the era of Buddhism, anything prior to the age of Buddhism may be described as pre-historical.

Prahmaha Term, from the Buddhapadipa Temple, Wimbledon, indicated that today there are no religious holidays *per se* for the lay-Buddhist. In Thailand, for example, the religious days were cancelled about thirty years ago, though local observation of certain 'feast' days continues, as does the intertwining of culture and religion. There are however, two days per month called *uposatha* days. These coincide with the full moon and new moon and are analogous to the Christian Sunday and the Jewish Shabbat in that they are special days of religious observance for both monks and lay-Buddhists. All the major Buddhist festivals, apart from New Year, are celebrated on full moon days. The fact that Buddhism in religious practice combines solar and lunar aspects means that calculation is difficult.

In observing the regular pattern of the lunar cycle there are four 'prayer days' in each month. Wan Pra is the name given to these prayer days, which by practice assume religious significance. Monks will observe additionally the three months of the rainy season as a period of religious significance even when living in the UK. It is observed as a time of study in Buddhism. The temple serves as the provider of, and focal point for, appropriate instruction for the monks.

Since the second world war Thailand, for example, has been heavily affected by Westernising influences. So the Buddhist New Year officially is now January 1st, although the traditional new year Song Kran will be observed on April 13th each year. Whilst there may be 4/5 weeks in April/May for the holiday period in Thailand, Buddhists will adopt the Western practice in the UK and there are no clashes with school term-times.

Table 6.1 outlines the main Buddhist festivals.

Table 6.1: Buddhist Festivals

	Name of the Festival				
	Wesak or Vaisakhi	Magha Puja	Vassa	Kathina	Loy Kratong
Date	Lunar: Full moon in May	Full moon February	3 months coincides with rainy season in SE Asia	October/November	October/November
Significance	Marks the life of the Buddha	Marks the 3 important events in the Buddha's life: disciples, rules and death	Time of fasting for monks who study/meditate strictly	Gratitude expressed to the monks for their religious role	Sharing of the spirit of the Buddha
Food	see written text				
Ritual	Cleanliness Decoration Worship at statue. Candle-lit processions	Temple based monks present candle-lit procession	Monks study and meditate	Cloth/clothing given to monks	Flower floating
Theme concepts	Key figure Celebration	Life of Buddha Followers, rules, death	Self-discipline	Gratitude	sharing

The calendar of Christianity

The Christian calendar traditionally has revolved around the birth date of its founder, Jesus Christ. Events before his birth are represented as BC or Before Christ, those subsequently AD (Latin: Anno Domini) meaning the 'year of Our Lord'. The fact that there was a mathematical error in determining the year of Christ's birth is of no real consequence. The Julian calendar with its inaccurate calculations was remedied by the introduction of the Gregorian calendar in 1752, although the Orthodox Church refused to adopt it and now celebrates its Church year 13 days behind the Western Church. This has implications for children of an Orthodox Church background. For example, Christmas is celebrated by Orthodox Christians on January 6th each year which is often after the commencement of the Spring teaching term.

The Gregorian calendar is solar. The phases of the moon are ignored, but leap year adjustments allow the lunar and solar phases to keep pace with each other. Within Christianity some dates are fixed so that they are repeated annually on the same date. Other festivals vary, reflecting origins elsewhere. Easter, for example, is a Christianised Passover feast which was always on a fixed day of the lunar month. Today the date of Easter is determined by the Paschal full moon which can fall any time between March 21st and April 25th. This of course affects Whitsuntide as well.

Christmas, celebrating the Incarnation of Jesus, always falls on December 25th, and the majority of Saints days are also fixed dates. So for example:

> the patron saint of England, St. George, is remembered on April 23rd.
> the patron saint of Ireland, St. Patrick, is remembered on March 17th.
> the patron saint of Wales, St. David, is remembered on March 1st.
> the patron saint of Scotland, St. Andrew, is remembered on November 30th.

It is not likely within the UK that a child would need to absent themselves from the classroom in order to attend a Christian Festival. Those who are likely to celebrate Saints days are those more likely to send their children to Church schools where these special dates would be recognised and celebrated within the school context.

Table 6.2: Christian Festivals

	Advent	Christmas	Lent	Mothering Sunday	Easter	Whitsun	Harvest
Additional/ Alternative Name		Birthday of Jesus Yuletide	Shrove Tues Ash Wednesday		Maundy Thur Good Friday Easter Sun	Pentecost	
Date	Nov/Dec	December 25	Feb/Mar April	March	Mar/April	7 Sundays after Easter	Sept/Oct
Significance	Preparation for Christmas	Birthday of Jesus	40 days in wilderness and prep. for Easter	Nurture of child by mother	Death and resurrection of Jesus	Holy Spirit received by disciples	Thanksgiving
Food		Turkey, mince-pies, plum-pudding Traditional meal	Fasting Give up delicacies		Hot cross buns, eggs, end of Lent Fish on Good Friday		Mainly farm produce given to needy
Ritual	Light advent candle; calendar	Decorate house, tree – lights Carols sung Nativity plays	Contemplation	Presents/ cards. Treats for Mum	Communion March of witness, special readings	Special readings, Church worship	Hymns and readings Giving parcels
Theme concepts	Light, hope	Gifts and giving, love, peace, light, joy	Self-discipline meditation food/fasting	Thankfulness parenthood sharing/giving	Life/death vicarious suffering forgiveness	Renewal of belief power	Thanksgiving Pattern/ seasons fruitfulness

Table 6.3: Hindu Festivals

	\multicolumn{7}{c	}{Name of the Festival}
	Ram Navami	Raksha Bandan	Krishna Janamashtami	Navaratri	Dussehra	Diwali	Holi
Alternative Name	Birthday of Rama		Birthday of Krishna	Durga Puja		Deepavali Festival of Lights	Spring Festival
Date	Chaitra Mar/April	Sravana July/August	Sravana July/August	Asvina 1–9 September/October	Asvina 10 September/October	Asvina September/October	Phalguna Feb/March
Significance	Birthday of Rama. Incarnation of Vishnu	Friendship ceremony of brothers/sisters	Birthday of Krishna. Incarnation of Vishnu	Celebrates Rama and Sita. Feast day of Durga	Rama defeats the demon Ravana	Various Good v evil Light New year	Phrahlad delivered from flames
Food	Fast day, no salt, cereals or vegetables	Sweet foods given	Fasting then feast in evening	Fasting and then meal of fruit		Diwali sweets. Fasting and feasting	Chapattis roasted coconut from fire
Ritual	Read the Ramayanas	Bracelets tied on wrists of male relations	Stay up late or all night	Dancing around statue of Durgha	Social gathering Effigies burnt	Diva lights decorations Rangooli Fireworks	Practical jokes fireworks bonfires
Theme concepts		friendship loyalty responsibility		Love	Loyalty Good triumphing over evil	Light New beginnings	Faith Joy Good/evil

The Hindu calendar

The reader should note that several calendars operate in India. For matters of civil administration there is reliance upon the Indian National calendar, which reflects the solar emphasis of the Gregorian calendar as well as the 'British' legacy in India. The religious or festival Hindu calendar is a luni/solar one. This reflects the nature of the moon. So the Purnimanta months begin with the dark fortnight (waning moon) and the Amanta months begin with the light fortnight (waxing moon). The former is Sanskrit and its operational in Northern India whilst the latter is Tamil, and is operational in Southern India. The implications of this are that different Hindu communities within the UK may well celebrate festive occasions on varying dates, depending on their origins.

The fact that the solar calendar has been influential in India since the fourth century CE reflects the emphasis on astrological factors within the Faith itself. It is not within the scope of this book, however, to record the methods of calculation for the balancing of lunar and solar days and the adjustments of months every few years.

The Islamic calendar

The Muslim calendar reflects the escape or flight of the Prophet Muhammad (pbuh) from Makkah to Madinah in the year Christians date as 622. Consequently events subsequent to this event are written AH which is the abbreviation for After *Hijrah* (the flight).

The simplest way of changing the dates from the Christian era to the Muslim is to use the formula:

$$AH = \frac{33}{32}(CE - 622) \text{ where } CE = \frac{32}{33}(AH) + 662$$

Exemplar:

$$2{,}000 \text{ CE} = \frac{33}{32}(2{,}000 - 622)$$

$$= \frac{33}{32}(1378) = 1421$$

Muslim festivals follow the Islamic calendar which is based on lunar months. This is shorter than the solar calendar by about 10 or 11 days. The Muslim calendar is therefore either 354 or 355 days. Festival dates are observed on the basis of the sightings of the moon. Within the UK several of the Muslim communities rely upon the Meteorological Office for accuracy of sightings.

Table 6.4: Muslim Festival Calendar

	Name of the Festival					
	Moharram	Maulid	Ramadhan	Lailat-Al-Qadr	Id-Ul-Fitr	Id-Al-Adha
Alternative Name	Hijra	Prophet's birthday	Month of fasting	Night of power	Breaking the fast Little festival	Feast of sacrifice Great festival
Date	Moharram	Rabi Al-Awwal	Ramadhan	Ramadhan	Shawwal	Zul-Hijja
Significance	Founding of Muslim community	Remember ministry of Muhammad (pbuh)	The Prophet began to receive revelations from God	First revelation of Qur'an from Gabriel	End of Ramadhan Thanksgiving to God for help during fast	Abraham's intended sacrifice of his son Ishmael
Food			One month fast during hours of daylight		Sweets for children. Break fast	Sacrifice animal for friends/relatives
Ritual	Greetings exchanged. Stories of the Prophet and his companions	Time for thanksgiving	Prayers at mosque. Disciplined pace of life plus fasting Read Qur'an	Qur'an read for previous ten days	New clothes General rejoicing Visit friends Mosque worship Almsgiving	Best clothes Mosque worship
Theme concepts			Sufferings of the poor and hungry. Rejoicing in the Qur'an		Friendship Sharing Helping the poor Forgive/forget	Sacrifice Obedience Pilgrimage

Table 6.5: The Muslim calendar months

1. Moharram	5. Jama Awal	9. Ramadhan
2. Safar	6. Jama Alsaniya	10. Shawwal
3. Rabi-Ul-Awwal	7. Rajab	11. Zul Qaada
4. Rabi-Us-Sani	8. Shaban	12. Zul Hijja

The Jewish calendar

The Jewish calendar, based on the phases of the moon, dates back to the year of the Creation of the world recorded in the Torah (Genesis chapter 1). So the Jewish years reflect AM (Latin: Anno Mondale), 'the year of the world'.

An example of this would be the display on a stone tablet over the entrance to the Bevis Marks synagogue in the City of London. This is the oldest synagogue in Britain and the stone tablet reflects a dual dating system. It reads

AM 5461 1701AD

therefore 2000 CE = AM 5460

Table 6.6: The Jewish months and their order

1. Nisan	5. Av	9. Kislev
2. Iyyar	6. Elul	10. Tevet
3. Sivan	7. Tishri	11. Shevat
4. Tammuz	8. Heshvan	12. Adar

The 'religious' New Year occurs in Tishri, the seventh month. The new year festival, *Rosh Hashanah*, marks the creation of the world. This is a different celebration to that of Nisan which is the lunar new year.

Jews generally tend to use a solar/lunar basis for their year. They use the moon for their basic calculations but adjust to the solar seasons when it becomes necessary.

The moon completes its cycle approximately every 29.5 days. As this is not a whole number some months are short of this and others are longer. The sighting of the new moon determines the new month. This period between months is called *Rosh Hodesh* and is marked by the sighting of the moon. To adjust for the solar calendar some months may have one or two days of Rosh Hodesh.

Such is the precision of dating adopted by the Jewish communities it is possible to purchase 100 year calendars.

Table 6.7: Jewish Festivals

	\multicolumn{8}{c}{Name of the Festival}
	Pesach	Shavuot	Rosh Hashanah	Yom Kippur	Sukkoth	Hannukah	Purim
Alternative Name	Passover. Feast of Unleavened Bread.	Pentecost. Feast of Weeks	New Year. Festival of the Trumpets	Day of Atonement	Feast of Tabernacles or Booths	Festival of Lights or Dedication	Feast of Lots or Feast of Esther
Date	Nisan 15th (Mar/April)	7 wks after Pesach	Sept/Oct	10 days after Rosh Hashanah	5 days after Yom Kippur Last 8 days	Nov/Dec 8 days duration	March
Significance	10 Plagues The Exodus	Ten commandments	Creation Patriarchs Judgment	Day of repentence Holiest day	Tabernacles in desert wanderings	Maccabean revolt. Temple re-dedicated	Esther's triumph over anti-semitism
Food	No leaven Seder meal		Bread, apples, honey	Fasting	Meals in Sukkah	Latkes biscuits	
Ritual	House cleaned Candle search Haggadah Seder	Floral decorations Book of Ruth read. Harvest gift	Shofar blown 10 days of penitence	Rabbi plus ark in white. Book of Jonah Shofar	Sukkah built Decorated fruit, evergreen leaves flowers	Hannukiyah lit over 8 days. Presents	Esther scroll read. Fancy dress games, gifts to poor
Theme concepts	Relationships Identity God with his people symbols	Rules Harvest Thanksgiving	Birthdays Sorrow Repetance	Clothes Colour Relationships	Wholeheartedness Dwellings Journeys	Light Faithfulness Loyalty Heroism	Games Charity Clothes Heroines

The Sikh calendar

Guru Nanak Dev Ji, the founder of Sikhism was born in 1469 CE. He, with others, worked out an equivalent dating system to the Western solar calendar but it was based on the phasing of the moon. The Sikh dating system, called Bikkarmi Sammat, is a lunar one, but employs as the base year, the year '0' in the Christian Era of dating. The year 1991 on the Bikkarmi Sammat system is 2047/2048.

For the Sikhs there are four main 'jugs', or eras of time, each with its own religious characteristics:

(1) Satjug. This is the time when, if an individual prayed, then the whole country received the benefit. If the individual were bad, then the whole country suffered. Mostly this was an era of peace.
(2) Tretajug. This is the time when, if the individual prayed, the whole region of the town/city received the benefit. If the individual wished harm on others then the town received the outcome. It was an era of contrast between loving and not loving. It was a time of Ravan, and warriors.
(3) Dupharjug. If a person prayed or was malicious then the immediate locality received it. The era was characterised by taypay, which was prayer to the Lord until he answered.
(4) Kalljug. This is the current era, in which if the individual does wrong then the outcome will be reaped on that individual.

The Sikh lunar calendar revolves around three main elements:

> Masya which is the New Moon,
> Purnmasi which is the Full Moon, and
> Sangrand which is the new month.

All are days on which special prayers will be said at the Gurdwara.

The Sikh Faith derives from the 10 Human Gurus as well as the *Guru Granth Sahib*, the Sikh scriptures. The birthdays (Awtar) and the days of the deaths (Jotijot) of the Gurus are celebrated, as well as the 'birthdate of the Guru Granth Sahib (Parkash). The collective name given to these days devoted to the Gurus is *Gupurbs*.

Other dates of significance are linked to the festivals of Lohree, Vaisakhi (or Baisakhi) and Raakhi (sisters day). Additionally there are days called Shahidi, which specially celebrate those who died in the place of others. This notion of vicarious suffering and death is linked to two of the Gurus, Guru Arjan Dev Ji (the fifth Guru) and Guru Teg Bahadur Dev Ji (the ninth Guru). The four Sikhs who died with the ninth Guru are also honoured with dates on the calendar called Sahib.

The significance of these dates to the community is expressed in the way they are celebrated. There are 'painful' days such as the Shahidi or Sahib, when people will generally go quietly. There are days of celebrating the lives and times of the Gurus. Happy days would include Lohree and Diwali.

Before all major days the Holy Book, The Guru Granth Sahib, will be read through non-stop. This will take three days and is usually commenced early in the morning, and the cycle of reading will finish also early in the morning of the holy day. The reading is called the *Akhand Path* and will take place in the *Gurdwara*. Additionally the Akhand Path may take place before a significant occasion such as a wedding or someone's twenty-first birthday, though the actual reading may be spread over seven days. Within the family and the Sikh community generally there will be other significant dates. For example, if it is the birthday of someone, then special prayers or Kirtan will be said at the Gurdwara on a subsequent date. This will also include a Langar Sewa (see Chapter 3 on diet).

Sad days obviously include funerals and special prayers are said at different stages in the ceremony. When the body is taken to the Temple then the Chopay Path is followed. This derives from the teachings of Guru Gobind Singh Dev Ji as well as his own experience of sufferings. The Sukhmani Sahib Path is a prayer deriving from Guru Arjan Dev Ji when prayerful requests are made for the soul of the deceased to receive the Lord's blessing.

Observing the anniversary date of the death of a parent will not involve food but special prayers will be said.

Table 6.8: The Western/Punjabi lunar calendar

January/February	= month of Maagh
February/March	= month of Phagun
March/April	= month of Chet
April/May	= month of Vaisaakh
May/June	= month of Jetth
June/July	= month of Haarh
July/August	= month of Saawan
August/September	= month of Bhaadon
September/October	= month of Assoo
October/November	= month of Kattak
November/December	= month of Magghar
December/January	= month of Poh

Table 6.9: Sikh Festivals

	Name of the Festival				
	Diwali	Birthday of Guru Nanak	Hola Mohalla	Baisakhi
Alternative Name	Festival of Lights		Holi	Vaisaakh
Date	Kattak Oct/Nov	Kattak Oct/Nov	Phagun Feb/March	Vaisaakh April 16
Significance	Release of G. Hargobind from Gwalior	Founder of Sikhism	Spring festival	Birthday of Khalsa
Food	Sweet foods communal meal	Communal meal	Communal meal	Communal meal
Ritual	Illuminations in Gurdwara Fireworks	Procession of holy book		Re-enactment of creation of Khalsa. New flag
Theme concepts	Light Good over evil Key figure	Birthdays Key figure	Games, tricks, colour	Symbol, identity belonging community

The Sikhs celebrate the birth and death days of all ten Gurus. These auspicious days are called Gupurbs. All these dates are accompanied by an Akhand Path cycle of readings.

Practical implications for celebrating festivals in school

The fundamental nature of a festival needs careful consideration as to whether it is appropriate to celebrate that festival in school. Can these festivals actually be celebrated in an authentic manner, or in 'diluting' them do we do a disservice to the Faith itself. Christmas is a good example of a festival which occurs annually and all too often distances children from the true nature of the festival itself. On a broader scale within society it has been secularised and commercialised and its essence glossed over. As teachers in the classroom we must balance our responsibilities towards the children we teach as well as the Faith we are considering.

Festivals within Faiths revolve around the family and the Faith community. The nature of festival dictates this. If we have children in our classroom from a variety of backgrounds, it is worth considering developing links with the family and Faith community whose festival is being considered. Aspects that could naturally be developed in the primary classroom would include foods, stories and crafts. This type of involvement enhances the dignity of the child who belongs to the relevant Faith as well as developing religious understanding at an appropriate level and linking school and home in a positive manner.

Work on festivals can find expression in the school assembly. The work that the children have attempted in the classroom can be explored within the broader school community. I have attended several Diwali assemblies where the children and staff have dressed up in, for example, saris, and celebrated the story with music, dance, drama and story. At the conclusion children distributed traditional foods made by parents on the school premises earlier in the day. The assembly hall was decorated with rangooli patterns made by the children as well as other pictures of the story. There was a sense of 'specialness' in these assemblies that brought the school community closer together. Care will need to be exercised by staff when celebrating a range of festivals. Many parents, especially if of a fundamental persuasion, may well express their objections to other religions being celebrated. Teachers must be clear in their own mind what they are attempting to do, bearing in mind that it is not the role of the county school to promote adherence to one religion *vis-à-vis* others.

Getting children to act out the stories in dramatic role play is a simple way of dealing with the story in an authentic and educationally justifiable manner without running the risk of antagonising parents who may feel apprehensive about celebrating festivals other than their own.

Festivals are an ideal opportunity to develop experiential RE whereby the children are encouraged to share in a genuine and authentic celebration as expressed by a Faith community. This is far different from proselytising or indoctrinating both of which are not allowed in the county school. The cognitive and affective aspects of RE may validly be explored.

The celebration of festivals helps reflect the community life of a school which over a period of time embraces the different members of the school community rather than leaving certain children on the outside. This, after all, will reflect the hidden curriculum and the stated aims of a school which will usually include valuing all children as part of the school community.

There is a need for staff planning over a period of years to reflect the cycle of festivals which portrays the variety of traditions within Britain today. This can be achieved as part of curriculum planning with forethought and sensitivity being practised.

CHAPTER 7

Customs, Courtesies and Sacred Objects

'Take off your shoes for you are treading on Holy ground' is a maxim that the classroom practitioner would do well to observe metaphorically unless undue offence is to occur. Blunders are often made unwittingly. It is not the blunders *per se* that usually cause the problems; it is more often the attendant insensitivity that is the source of offence, if the problem is ignored. The classroom teacher, regardless of his or her own religious, or non-religious, persuasion, has a lifetime of learning if pupils and religions are not to be stereotyped and tokenism exhibited.

This chapter has two purposes. The first is to consider traditional customs or courtesies that would be helpful for teachers when visiting various places of worship, or in meeting members of other Faiths. Some of these customs are required of the lay-community of the Faith as well as general visitors, while others are optional to the visitor from outside the Faith yet will be noted as a mark of respect by those from within. The teacher might like to ensure that children visiting these places of worship are taught these requirements. The second purpose is to weigh up the general and the specific issues relating to the classroom usage of religious artefacts from different Faiths.

There are some who would argue that artefacts from different religions should not be present in the classroom. Others argue that there should be no limitations placed on the use of artefacts in the classroom. The view taken here is that artefacts are useful if used with discretion and sensitivity. Reference has already been made to sacred writings and the classroom in Chapter 5 so this aspect is not considered here.

Buddhism

A typical Asian greeting is to place the hands together in front of the chest and to bow slightly with the head or upper body. This type of greeting was taught by the Buddha and is common across the Indian sub-continent. When lay-Buddhists meet each other a typical comment would be 'Sawaddee...' which means 'Good...'. If they were addressing a woman they would add 'Kah' which means 'Ms'. If they were addressing a man they would add 'Krub' which is the equivalent of 'Sir'.

It is likely that if they were talking to a monk they would initially address him by saying 'Namaskarn' meaning 'respect to you'. Titles of learning and office include terms such as 'Phrah' or 'Phramaha'. These reflect the study and scholarship of the individual monk as well as reflecting their status within the *sangha*, the name given to the monastic community. Deference is always paid to the leader of the sangha who has the title of Superior or Abbot.

If a woman is meeting a monk it should be remembered that one of the monk's Precepts is to avoid physical contact with women. It would be inappropriate therefore to offer the hand in a handshake. The typical greeting described above would be appropriate and preferable.

When visiting a Buddhist temple (the collective term for all the various religious buildings within an area is Wat), it is usual practice for visitors to remove their shoes prior to entry. This is a simple matter of respect, as well as one of practical cleanliness. Devotees sit on the floor which therefore has to be kept clean. The shrine which is usually higher than the devotee is symbolic of the authority and position of the Buddha as a teacher of eminence.

At the temple it is common for the lay-Buddhists to come and express their own devotions which may include the lighting of jos sticks, prostrating and bowing as well as meditating quietly. Meditation can take various forms including walking and sitting. The devotee may even use the visit as the occasion to give food gifts to the monastic community, the sangha. They will seek advice on many spiritual matters from the monks.

There are various Buddhist artefacts that may suitably be used in the classroom, or to form part of a display. A statue of the Buddha may well depict various body and hand positions which reflect symbolically aspects of the Faith.

Other artefacts which could be shown include a prayer wheel, or a rosary (string of beads) which is used by certain Buddhist groups, as is the mandala which is a symmetrical diagram built around a central point. Most Buddhists will also use incense sticks placed in a holder. It is quite common for temples to be decorated with wall paintings showing scenes from the life of the Buddha. Many families will use traditional-styled posters as part of their displays venerating the life of the Buddha. These too can form part of display work in school, as can various photographs. I have used paper flowers made by the children, when considering the festival of Loy Kratong. This is a festival when the community float paper flowers, jos sticks and candles, on lakes, ponds and rivers, to celebrate the life of the Buddha.

Christianity

There are great variations in customs across the Christian denominations. For instance, there is no single general greeting adopted by Christians. Some may wish each other 'the peace of the Lord' but this is not uniformly adopted. Variations might include 'God bless you' or 'God be with you'. However there are traditions when addressing a cleric of a particular type so an appropriate form of address is adopted. For example, a Bishop when being addressed might be called 'your grace' just as a vicar might be called 'father', or in Nonconformist circles he or she might be called 'Pastor'. It would be useful for the teacher to ascertain how the cleric would prefer to be addressed by children when they meet. Some prefer and expect formal terms to be used whilst others have adopted a more casual style.

It should be remembered when taking children to a church that it is a sacred place. The architecture of some churches is purposefully designed to create a sense of awe and wonder in the mind of the visitor. The position of the altar often opposite the entrance acts as a focal point. The high or vaulted ceilings with pillars are designed not only for acoustical purposes but also heighten feelings and sensations of personal insignificance when compared to the grandeur of God. Other churches deliberately have simplicity of design so that the sense of the sacred comes from within the worshipper. Certain Nonconformist groups such as the Quakers emphasise this. They have no clergy and dispense with images, altars and even musical instruments. They will not even have a purpose-built church, but regard the room as a 'meeting place' for their community, which they call the Society of Friends. The teacher should be aware that these divergent styles within the Christian Faith are deliberate.

If children are taken into a church, certain customs may need to be observed. Children may be tempted to test the echoing acoustics at the earliest opportunity, often in a manner not suited for the place! It is therefore often helpful to seat them quietly at the start so that they can gain a sense of their surroundings. The teacher must decide who is to talk to the children. Not all adults can communicate easily to children and so the teacher should be aware of this.

The teacher will also need to decide what the visit is trying to achieve. It is best not to attempt too much on one occasion. Many visits are ruined by not having a point of focus clearly enough defined and discipline issues arise.

Christianity has many associated artefacts but these may not all be used by any one denomination. Some churches will use *ikons*, or images, which may be used in the home as well. This is a popular item for the Orthodox community and serves, according to Father Mike Yannatos at St. John the Theologian, in Hackney, as a reminder of the example set by others for Christians to follow. The ikon itself is not worshipped but the people depicted are venerated as those whose example should help Christians to follow in their footsteps.

Very many Christians wear a symbol of Christianity in the form of a cross or a crucifix. This is a symbol of identity as well as a symbolic reminder to live the Christian life, though it is often worn simply as jewellery by many who are not even Christians. The rosary, or row of beads, is traditionally used in some denominations, especially Roman Catholics, as an aid to prayer. For some the crucifix may be part of the rosary.

Many Christians, particularly Anglicans, will use not only the Bible as an aid to worship but also may use a prayer book to accompany both services in the Church and private devotions at home.

The range of artefacts associated with Christianity, used both in the home and Church, is varied. The reader should make contact with those shops which supply goods for the Church. From these they can supply a variety of candles, cards and other objects that may be used in display work in the classroom.

Hinduism

Hindu greetings are similar to those of Buddhism whereby the hands are placed together in front of the chest with a slight bowing with the head and upper body. Garlanding is also a typical greeting for visitors amongst Hindus. The term 'namaste' may be used which simply means 'hello' or 'greetings'.

For the Hindu there are four main dimensions to life:

- Arta: basic or mundane needs,
- Karma: desires,
- Dharma: ethical or religious ideals,
- Moksha: spiritual salvation or liberation.

Often these are tied into the varying stages of a person's life so there may be varying expectations of an individual depending on their age and maturity. Most Hindu families will have a shrine at home for private devotions. It may be housed in a separate room or in the corner of a room. The regularity of devotion, called puja, will depend on the family practices or individual expressions of devotion. Washing prior to puja is normal. In terms of family roles, it is the women who usually ensure that the family's religious devotions are carried out. The religious education and upbringing of the children is seen predominantly as part of the mother's role.

Hinduism is rich in its imagery and its emphasis on the senses in worship. Therefore it is to be expected that a variety of sacred objects may be used in both the home and the temple. These range from incense, idols and bells to different types of food and flame. To exemplify this, a simple puja uses at least four elements associated with the idea of harvest. Water is used, symbolising the absence of drought; a flower may be presented to the god, symbolising happiness for the god and the worshipper; fruit is offered as a symbol of harvest and plenty; whilst light is offered symbolising understanding. The sheer breadth of Hinduism allows for a more general type of classroom display of which religion is only an element. General displays on India, its products such as teas, places and animals, such as the elephant, are also of relevance.

When visiting a Hindu temple, shoes are removed at the door prior to entry. Shoe racks are usually provided for this purpose. The teacher should give careful thought to the issue of who should talk to the group of children visiting the temple. Often the Brahmin priests are busy and English may not be their first language. Many temples will have non-priests as the point of reference either for taking bookings or to give talks to the children. It is likely when taking children to the temple that there will be devotees offering private puja or having a private ceremony with the priest. This will not necessarily interrupt an educational trip, rather it will add emphasis to it showing the dynamic nature of the temple and the people who use it.

Islam

Salaam meaning 'peace', is a traditional Muslim salutation. It is also customary to shake hands when greeting someone. A suitable response is to wish peace upon the person themselves by responding with 'salaam alayakum'. The term has the same root as 'Islam' itself which means 'submission' or 'obedience' to Allah from whom true peace is derived.

For Muslims the purpose of life itself is to worship and do the will of Allah. Therefore, whatever action is being carried out, is to please Allah. The basic religious requirements are called the *Five Pillars of Islam*:

(1) *Shahadah*, which is the declaration of faith.
(2) *Salah*, which are the five compulsory daily prayers. These may be offered individually or corporately. The five times are fixed to certain periods of the day. These are:

   (a) from dawn until just before sunrise
   (b) after mid-day until early afternoon
   (c) late afternoon until just before sunset
   (d) after sunset until daylight ends
   (e) night time until midnight or dawn

(3) *Zakat*, which is welfare contribution. This may be paid once a year from savings, and may be in the form of cash or jewellery. Usually 2.5 per cent of the savings will be given. It is a compulsory levy and therefore is not seen as charity. Charity is over and above this amount.
(4) *Hajj*, which is the pilgrimage to Makkah.
(5) *Sawm*, which is fasting during the month of Ramadhan. The purpose behind this practice is to develop self-control and help to overcome faults such as selfishness and greed. With its abstentions Sawm helps keep hunger, comfort and sex under control.

Shar'iah is the code of law for all Muslims. The term means 'example' or 'clear path'. Conduct rests on two sources – the Qur'an, revealed by Allah and the Sunnah which are the teachings of the Prophet. In combination, these two texts give Muslims a complete basis for practical living. The principles are enunciated in the Qur'an and the details are elucidated in the Sunnah. The importance and influence of Shar'iah will affect the Muslim child in the classroom in terms of attitude and conduct.

Islam traditionally does not allow free mixing of grown-up boys and girls, nor does it allow sex outside of marriage. Boy-friend/girlfriend relationships are therefore not approved, nor are mixed parties. The majority of Muslims with daughters of secondary school age will choose a single-sex school rather than one that was co-educational. G. Sarwar, (1982) in *Islam Beliefs and Teachings* (MET), states that Muslims are not allowed to have a shower in the nude in the presence of others. Teachers must be sensitive to this code of practice in PE/swimming classes at school, especially if the children are slightly older. Teachers may wish to discuss these matters with parents.

Religious artefacts that are used at home may suitably be used by the teacher in the classroom. The prayer mat is used five times daily. It may have floral or geometric patterning of the kind that is so characteristic of Islam. Some of these mats may have a built-in compass so that the direction of Makkah can be ascertained accurately. Children find this of great interest in working out bearings. Worshippers, male and female, cover their heads when praying and many differing styles of head-dress have developed. These items allow for a variety of curricular approaches to be adopted whilst considering aspects of Islam.

When visiting a mosque, visitors must always remove their shoes and place them in a rack near to the entrance. This is because during prayer time worshippers perform a series of prostrations, called Raka'hs, and the floor needs to be kept clean. Prior to entering the mosque both men and women will cover their heads. They will usually pray separately so that natural distractions are minimised and the reason for worship is not hindered in any way. Some mosques have screens, balconies or even separate halls for the women. Many non-Muslims are surprised at the simplicity of a mosque. It may have floral or geometric patterning but beyond that it is usually very plain with carpeting and no seats (except for those who are handicapped in some way). The fact that all worshippers prostrate together means that there is equality before God amongst the worshipping community. When meeting the Imam, the leader of the mosque female visitors should not offer a handshake.

Judaism

Shalom, which means 'peace', is a traditional Jewish greeting. The peace referred to is that which is derived from living one's life according to the standards of God. Shalom also reinforces Jewish feelings of identity and a special interpersonal relationship. This is the most common form of Jewish greetings.

When visiting a synagogue with children males will be required to wear a head covering. It is often an interesting craft activity to get the boys to make and decorate a suitable 'yamelkah', or Jewish skull cap, although paper ones will probably be available on arrival. If the visit does not coincide with a service, then it is unlikely even in an orthodox synagogue, that boys and girls would need to be separated.

Judaism is rich in traditions and symbols. Consequently the artefacts in use in the home and synagogue are diverse and numerous. Many of these are appropriate as a means of teaching about Judaism in the classroom, and can include the following. The symbol of the old Temple in Jerusalem is the Menorah, the seven-pronged candlestick. Mention in the chapter on calendars, has been made to Hannukah and the eight-pronged menorah, called the Hannukiyah, used at this annual festival.

Reference has also been made to the Bar Mitzvah ceremony when the boy will wear the two phyllacteries, one on the left upper arm and the other on the forehead. These act as a constant reminder of the presence of God. These phyllacteries are worn for daily personal prayers. They contain the words of the *Shema*. Male Jews will always wear the kappel, or yamelkah, when in the synagogue or when praying at home.

Teachers could also make reference to food packages which reflect that the contents are *Kosher* (see chapter on diet). The festival of Passover with the *Seder* dish and prescribed order of the meal can also prove a valuable artefact for the classroom. There are also the various covers for the breads used at *Shabbat* and Passover.

Sikhism

When meeting Sikhs they will greet each other with the words 'sat sri Akaal'. This means 'greetings to God (the creator)'. The concept within the greeting is that God is creator and the individual being addressed, belongs to God. Accompanying this is the typical form of Asian greeting whereby the hands are placed together in front of the chest together with a slight bowing of the head and upper body.

When visiting the Gurdwara with children it should be noted that head coverings should be worn when entering the prayer hall, additionally the shoes should be removed. There are shoe racks near to the entry for this purpose There are no chairs in the prayer hall, and all devotees sit on the floor. The removal of shoes is a matter of hygiene. The covering of the head is out of respect for God and His sacred writings, which are rested upon a raised dais under a canopy. The symbol here is that the worshipper sits beneath the holy writings signifying that there is no higher authority on earth. Sikhs will usually kneel and bow, so that the forehead touches the floor before the sacred writings, thus showing personal respect for God. This more elaborate form of respect is not required of non-Sikhs. However, children visiting the Gurdwara should respect the tradition that prior to sitting down in the prayer hall the presence of God is acknowledged by bowing in a simplified manner. This can be achieved by placing the hands together in front of the chest and bowing slightly from the head or upper chest. Children may be invited to look at the sacred writings but should never touch the sacred text.

Mention has been made in Chapter 4 of the 5 K's worn by Sikhs. These are of course artefacts of the Sikh religion as they are symbolic of the Faith itself. Whilst four of these items are appropriate for the classroom in terms of introducing the Faith, one is probably not. It may prove sensible not to have the *kaccha*, or baggy underwear, in the classroom or the possibility of ridicule may arise. This may prove damaging to a Sikh child if he or she is in the classroom or the child may be teased later, for example, in the playground.

Other artefacts may include a prayer book, posters of some of the Gurus, or some of the forms of head covering or clothing.

Practical implications for the teacher

Given careful preparation by the teacher, the value of an educational visit to places of worship should never be underestimated, since it will help children to respect members of the Faith and to gain greater understanding of religious practices.

Wherever one is in the UK there is always a nearby place of worship. Many teachers who have not included religious visits as part of their RE would do well to have a familiar starting point, and for many that may well be the local parish church.

Whatever the type of place of worship visited, there are some general principles and guidelines that are worth considering. These are apart from the usual LEA and school policies for journeys or financial and practical travel arrangements.

The timing of a visit is of great importance. Is it convenient for the school, and the group being taught, and is it appropriate to the teaching programme being undertaken?

The level of parental involvement is of key importance in religious education. Many teachers involve parents as part of general practice, especially in primary schools. Parents from a particular Faith, if available, may be the ones to be most appropriately involved in visiting a place of worship with which they are familiar as a worshipper. Such parents could be helpful in preparation for the visit.

The aim behind an RE visit needs to be clearly thought through. It has implications for language development, and should inform any preparatory work to tell the children what to expect and how they should behave appropriately. A teacher is advised to visit the place prior to taking children there.

On arrival, the teacher should ensure that appropriate customs are adopted. The teacher should be clear about what form of talk by a member of the Faith would be appropriate. Some adults find it difficult to talk to children at their level, but the teacher can adopt practical ways of ensuring that the speaker refers to what the teacher requires. This can be achieved by the children having questions ready to ask. Or it could be that a parent of one of the children be invited to talk with the class and show them around the place of worship. This means that parents are there not only to support the visit but also to contribute positively from that particular Faith perspective.

The teacher should also consider whether the visit is to act as a catalyst for subsequent work, whether it is to consolidate past work, or whether it represents the climax of a topic. This will influence whether a display or presentation, assembly contribution or even a subsequent visit are deemed appropriate.

CHAPTER 8

Non-theistic Stances and Christian Sects

In a book of this nature it is not possible to reflect the full extent of religious diversity to be found in our classrooms. Sometimes this is because sects and stances are numerically small or fairly localised in extent. Rather than try to cover all these, this chapter concentrates on one example of what may be termed, a non-theistic stance for living, and on one example of a Christian sect. Both are commonly represented in schools in the UK. The reader is urged to note the effect of both on their professional role, and extend this awareness to other groups which are not dealt with in this book.

Humanism as an example of a non-theistic stance for living

Humanism is an important example of a non-theistic stance for living. Non-theistic is a term applied to a religion, or approach to life style, that does not include a deity (from some aspects this term applies also to Buddhism with its absence of a deity), but which displays many other aspects of religion that are readily identifiable. The characteristic qualities which sociologists identify as religion may be found in, and applied to, the Humanist movement. Humanism is ancient, dynamic and portrays the main dimensions of religion. The nature of Humanism however, does not easily fit the structure of this book, so this section has been added at the end of the book rather than partially being dealt with in sections in each chapter. Its position here is not one of relegation, however, but merely reflects the practical problems of placing it in earlier chapters.

Within Humanism there is a great breadth of thought and practice, as there is within any of the world's Faiths. Whilst there are those who have adopted an apparently militant stance, for example attacking the privileges afforded to the Church by the State, there are other Humanists who are fairly closely linked with religious groups, for example the Quakers. In brief there is no such thing as a typical Humanist, though there are some common attitudes and beliefs.

John White, for the British Humanist Association (BHA), comments that 'all Humanists are individualists because of the engagement of the mind and the agnostic attitudes which are applied not only to ultimate questions but also to interpreting them in one's life'. This of course allows individuals to exercise control over their own lives and conduct. Due attention is paid by Humanists to the claim of Socrates when he stated, 'The unexamined life is not worth living'.

There is a developing tendency within the Humanist tradition to recognise the importance of rites and rituals within the life of the individual. There are now a series of BHA publications written by Jane Wynne Wilson which explore the rites of naming ceremonies, marriages and funerals from a non-religious perspective.

The role of a Humanist parent includes, what Brock Wilson describes as 'our responsibility...to help our children learn things and learn in ways that were not available to us when we were children'. A comment by Laurie Lee, in *The Firstborn*, emphasises this independence of each child as an individual when he states, 'She is a child of herself and will be what she is. I am merely the keeper of her temporary helplessness...'.

This independence of spirit is reflected in the words of Kahlil Gibran that could be included, and used, at a Humanist naming ceremony,

> Your children are not your children.
> They are the sons and daughters of Life's longing for itself.
> They come through you but not from you
> And though they are with you, yet they belong not to you.

Further on in the suggested ceremony come the words:

> If a child lives with tolerance she learns to be patient:
> If a child lives with encouragement, she learns confidence:
> If a child lives with praise, she learns to appreciate:
> If a child lives with fairness, she learns judgement:
> If a child lives with acceptance and friendship, she learns to give love to the world.

Throughout their lives, Humanists place great emphasis on the role of the individual in relation to understanding, conduct and responsibilities. For instance, there is an acceptance of the principle that natural resources are not inexhaustible, and so a careful exercise of responsibility should be exercised. In matters of diet the onus is on the individual to act according to their own conscience. Many Humanists are concerned about environmental issues and as a result are vegetarian on grounds of conscience.

Attitudes towards clothing and appearance tend to be similar to those adopted by the Quakers. Concern is expressed about the exploitation behind current fashion trends as well as a general concern about the conspicuous.

In relation to language and sacred writings, there is no belief in what may be described by others as 'revealed' truth. At the same time, respect is shown to the great minds of the past and particularly those within the Humanist tradition such as Epicurus, Thomas Paine, Pandit Jawaharial Nehru and Bertrand Russell, to name but a few.

The calendar for the Humanist recognises a human, rather than theistic, response to the natural environment and the turning of the year. For example, New Year is celebrated, rather than Christmas. The occasion serves as a reminder of the emergence of earlier humanity which rejoiced that the sun was going to 'come back again' and this was seen as a suitable time for a celebration. Increasingly today, United Nations day, held annually in June, is being seen by Humanists as a focal point to celebrate the interdependence of humanity.

Whilst Humanists do not have special customs or a specific set of rules for behaviour, the Golden Rule is adopted, 'Do unto others as you would have them do unto you'. Indeed, this principle permeates all the great religions as well as non-theistic stances for living. For the Humanist, it is an important matter to live out these ideals in practice.

Mention has already been made that Humanists do not have sacred texts or many of the rituals associated with conventional religion, so are there artefacts that could be representative of Humanism which could be used in the classroom? John White felt that the fossil was a suitable symbol of Humanism. An accompanying comment could be to the following effect, 'This was living two million years ago... Humanists believe it is part of an evolutionary process, of which we too are a part.'

In the classroom Humanists welcome an openness being extended not only to other Faiths but also to the non-theistic stances for living. John White comments, 'Humanists hope that teachers will exercise a great sensitivity to different world views, with each of them being equally respected'. Humanists feel that there are a variety of answers to questions of life, each of which is valid. For the Humanist, good RE is open, for Humanists, therefore, the greatest areas of concern revolve around the Act of Worship as required by the 1988 Education Reform Act. This is because the idea of worship makes assumptions which are both presumptuous and indoctrinatory, since the concept of worship implies particular beliefs which the children may not hold.

Jehovah's Witnesses as an example of a Christian sect

This religious group are often victims of media distortion, with their views on blood transfusions being offered as an example of inhumanity and eccentricity. There are many 'witnesses', as adherents call themselves, to be found in the state classrooms and a brief summary of their position needs considering.

The Witnesses are an international body to be found in more than 200 countries. Their version of the Bible is central to daily living. It is both a focal- and reference-point for matters of belief and ethical conduct. The reader should find detailed information about the movement from the Witnesses themselves who have their own publishers called the Watchtower Bible and Tract Society.

Witnesses are often obvious in the classroom because of their reluctance to join in certain school activities. They certainly would not participate in an act of worship or the singing of school songs. The parents will therefore invariably exercise their right of withdrawal from religious worship and education, as embodied in the 1988 Education Reform Act. The refusal to participate in school songs reflects the conviction that total allegiance should be directed only to God and must not be tarnished by other concepts and loyalties being introduced. So, patriotic songs such as the National Anthem, would also be shunned. If a school were involving the children in political education then Witnesses would also withdraw from such involvement. So for example, learning the democratic processes through active participation in voting for class monitors or for classroom rules would cause a Witness not to participate. Whilst school termly patterns are totally linked to the calendar of festivals within the UK, Witnesses object to the celebration of these because in many instances they reflect non-Christian origins. The fact that they have been 'Christianised' is insufficient, and Witnesses withdraw totally from their celebration. (The Biblical basis for this action is taken from II Corinthians chapter 6 verses 14–17.) Likewise, birthdays are shunned because of the two references to parties cited in the Bible, both of which had negative results. This does not mean that Witnesses do not enjoy parties or the giving of gifts, they would not indulge in either outside of their community.

Anything which detracts from a life where Jehovah is central is to be shunned. Jehovah is the name they use for God. Witnesses generally do not participate in extra-curricular activities since re-creation tends instead to be organised by the families and within the general life of this believing community.

Schools adopting a sex-education programme as part of a Health Education policy should note the concerns of Witnesses, that sex education without a biblical basis is not considered suitable for their children. Likewise a Science curriculum that teaches evolution as exclusive truth is regarded as being in direct conflict with the creation story in the Bible and is therefore rejected. Music and Art, if linked to festivals or any religious matter, would also be rejected by Witnesses. Where the PE curriculum includes any form of martial arts, training in this too would prove to be unacceptable, as it cuts across the principle of living peacefully with all men.

That some of these issues seem to paint a negative picture of Witnesses is rather unfortunate. They have a positive attitude towards education generally, and will positively support a school and its teachers, as long as there is no conflict with their own beliefs and religious ethics. Where teachers have concerns, then dialogue with the parents will prove of value.

Practical implications for teachers

As part of their professional responsibility, teachers have to assist the child in the classroom to develop as an individual capable of making informed personal choices. This is fairly fundamental within our broad-based education system which may be classified as both liberal and critical. Some groups such as the Muslims and Jehovah's Witnesses find this position fundamentally flawed and would seek to offset it. Groups such as the Humanists would have no difficulty in being open and critical and see this as desirable. It is therefore necessary for teachers to find out about the nature of beliefs and their impact on attitude and conduct as they affect the classroom. Most theistic and non-theistic groups will have designated personnel responsible for suitable publications to inform those outside of the tradition. Many groups will have either an education officer or suitable educational publications, which can be obtained by teachers for their own information or for use in the classroom. The parents of the child in the classroom may prove a useful starting point for dialogue and the obtaining of printed information.

CHAPTER 9
Conclusion

This book is only a beginning in the search for a greater understanding and appreciation of the importance of Faith to the individual believer, its transmission within the family and the implications within the classroom.

Since the Second World War there has been an extensive range of new religious movements developing within the UK. By the end of the 1980s the number of these new movements was nearly five hundred. Some of these are quite obscure and localised yet distinctive enough to have their own ethical systems based on their beliefs. Several universities within the UK now have, within their theology faculty, a department of 'New Religious Movements', to whom the reader can refer. This book has not attempted to consider these variations though they may increasingly affect the classroom practitioner and cause perplexity. As there will always be marked local variations, the reader is encouraged to follow up some of the comments within this book and ascertain their relevance for his or her own situation.

It is hoped that this book will have helped the reader to challenge any stereotypical thinking that may have existed, even if it was in the subconscious mind. The difference in the range of beliefs and practice between successive generations has had a noticeable effect on the classroom and no doubt will continue to do so.

In researching this book I have found it a challenge to find what I shall describe as 'the authentic voice'. The vastness and scale of religion is such that it is hard to find a norm within any one tradition. The effect within the classroom is that teachers may be tempted to generalise, but they must ensure that beliefs which depart from those commonly held are treated with understanding and sensitive awareness. Teachers should never guess or make up answers as the children question about religion. It is always helpful when asked a question, to which you do not know the answer, to admit the fact and encourage the children to find out, whilst you do the same.

I was conscious in writing this book that the term 'sensitivity' was repeatedly used and herein I believe lies the key to future development. Teachers should not expect to become experts in all religions, nor those outside teaching for that matter. They can however show an empathetic awareness of the nature of religion and its demands on the adherent. Sometimes, for children growing up, this will cause many types of internal conflict as the child seeks to discover his or her own identity in an age of rapid change. Religious Education should enable pupils to develop a knowledge and understanding of their own Faith and also learn to respect the beliefs of others. I hope this book may make some small contribution to this enterprise.

Glossary

Key to religions

(B) Buddhism (H) Hinduism (J) Judaism (C) Christianity (I) Islam (S) Sikhism

Abishekam (H) — A child naming ceremony which takes place in the temple and includes the washing of the deity.

Adhan or Azan (I) — The words whispered in both ears of a baby at birth. The words declare the central credal statement of Islam that there is no God but Allah and that Muhammad (PBUH) is His messenger. It also forms part of the daily call to prayer.

Adi Granth (S) — This literally means 'First Book'. The term dates from 1604 when the fifth Guru Arjan Dev Ji compiled his own sayings plus previous four Gurus, as well as other contributors.

Ahimsa (H) — This is the Hindu principle of non-violence being adopted, in the belief that the after-effects will adversely affect the one who is violent.

Akhand Path (S) — The term used for the non-stop reading of the Sikh scriptures. This will take three days to complete and is usually timed to finish when an auspicious occasion commences, eg. a festival. This may be performed by volunteers or a paid team.

Amrit (S) — The term commonly given to the sweet liquid used during various Sikh rituals.

Angel of Death (J) — This is associated with the events of the Passover when the firstborn Egyptians were killed by the Angel of Death. Biblical account recorded in Exodus chapter 12.

Aqeeqah (I) — The Muslim head shaving ceremony when a baby is one week old. It is accompanied by gifts of food and possibly money to the poor. The event may involve a family celebration.

Ark (J) — The name currently given to the receptacle on the East wall of every synagogue in which the Torah, the sacred scriptures, is housed.

Artanai (H) — A shorter form of the Hindu naming ceremony where only the names are recited.

Askenazi (J)	The term applied to those Jews who originated from central and Eastern Europe.
Bar Mitzvah (J)	The name given to the initiation rite for Jewish males on the sabbath after his thirteenth birthday. This rite includes reading publicly from the Torah. After successful completion of the rite the boy is viewed as an adult member of the religious community.
Bat Mitzvah (J)	The name given to the initiation rite for Jewish girls after their twelfth birthday. In some cases it may be at home or in the Reform tradition it may occur in the synagogue.
Bhikkus (B)	The name given to the order of monks founded by Gautama, the Buddha.
Bhog (S)	A term literally meaning 'pleasure' marking the end of the Akhand Path cycle of readings.
Brahmin (H)	(see caste) There are four varnas or Hindu social classes, of which the Brahmins are the highest. Their role is to transmit the ancient sanskrit traditions as well as performing the priestly role.
Brit Milah (J)	The Jewish rite of male circumcision on the eighth day after birth. It is symbolical of the covenant relationship between God and the descendants of Abraham.
Carnival (C)	A period of festival prior to Lent, especially in Roman Catholic countries.
Caste (H)	The social status inherited by Hindus at birth. Originally it was of a social character rather than a religious one.
Chism (C)	Sacred oil sometimes used to anoint the forehead with the sign of the cross in a Christening ceremony.
Christening (C)	Christian name-giving rite which admits a person to membership of the Church.
Dasam Granth (S)	Means the Last Granth, contains the teachings of the tenth Guru and various other writers.
Easter (C)	The principal Christian Festival celebrating the vicarious suffering of Jesus and His resurrection.
Eucharist (C)	The term which means 'thanksgiving', is an alternative term for sacrament also sometimes called the 'mass' or communion service.
Five Pillars (I)	These are fundamental practices required of Muslims. They include: repeating the creed, praying five times a day, giving alms, fasting and the pilgrimage to Makkah.
Gautama (B)	The clan name of the human prince commonly called the Buddha, because he achieved enlightenment. Born 560 BCE.

Gayatri Mantra (H)	A verse from the Rig Veda, regarded as particularly sacred to Hindus.
Grace (C)	A short thanksgiving offered to God either before or after a meal.
Granthi (S)	Meaning 'reader', the granthi is a spiritual Sikh leader within the Gurdwara whose responsibility will be in caring for the Guru Granth Sahib as well as the spiritual welfare of members.
Gupurb (S)	The name given by Sikhs to the celebration of either the birth or death day of one of the ten human Gurus.
Gurdwara (S)	Literally means 'the door of the Guru'. In its strictest sense this is wherever the sacred book, the Guru Granth Sahib, is kept.
Guru (S)	A term which for many Hindus refers to a human teacher. Within Sikhism it indicates the inner voice of God. The ten human Gurus of Sikhism are vehicles for the transmission of God's truth. They epitomised the presence of God.
Guru Gobind Singh Dev Ji (S)	The tenth and final human Guru who founded the Khalsa or community of Sikhs. He lived 1666–1708.
Guru Granth Sahib (S)	Also known as the Adi Granth or First Book, these are the Sikh scriptures. The entire volume is written in gumurki, the script used for modern Punjabi. The writings are the physical embodiment of the eternal Guru and treated with total reverence.
Guru Nanak (S)	Founder and first Guru of Sikhism (lived 1469–1539). Established Sikh principles, rejecting aspects of Hinduism and Islam.
Hadith (I)	Meaning 'tradition', this is a record of the sayings and stories associated with the life and teaching of the Prophet Muhammad (pbuh). The hadith forms part of Shariah, the sacred law of Islam.
Haggadah (J)	The name given to the hymns and stories told during the seder meal at Passover time.
Hajj (I)	One of the Five Pillars. It is the pilgrimage to Makkah, at least once in a Muslim's lifetime.
Hajji (I)	The name that can be adopted by one who has successfully completed hajj.
Halal (I)	A term which denotes that something is permissible because it conforms to Islamic requirements and rituals.
Haram (I)	Opposite of halal.
Hijab or Purdah (I)	Is the covering dress required of Muslim women.
Hijrah (I)	Means 'flight' and marks the migration of Muhammad from Makkah to Medina in 622 CE. Muslim calendar dates from this event, hence AH.

Id ul Adha (I)	Festival occurring during the Muslim hajj or pilgrimage.
Id ul Fitr (I)	Festival celebrated on the first day after the end of Ramadhan, the Muslim month of fasting.
Ikon (C)	A devotional picture or painting which is used as an aid to worship especially in the Christian Orthodox Churches.
Kaccha (S)	Baggy shorts worn by Sikhs as a symbol of moral behaviour and self-control.
Kangha (S)	Comb used and worn by Sikhs as a symbol of disciplining the mind as well as the body.
Kara (S)	The bracelet worn by Sikhs. Part of the 5 K's, it symbolises the Oneness of God and the unity of the community (the Khalsa).
Karah Prasad (S)	Food made from equal parts of wheat-flour, sugar and ghee, distributed in the Gurdwara at the end of all significant rituals. All members of the congregation eat this together. It symbolises sharing and unity.
Karma (H)	Central Hindu belief that any action will directly affect a consequence in one's lifetime or in subsequent rebirths.
Kashrut (J)	A code stating which foods may be eaten by Jews and how they should be prepared.
Kaur (S)	The female title meaning princess, given to Sikh initiates. Given at infancy the title is usually retained whether a lady is single or married.
Kesh (S)	The term given to the uncut hair which symbolises spirituality and respect for natural law among Sikhs.
Khanda (S)	An important Sikh emblem. It is a two-edged sword symbolising the temporal and the spiritual. The khanda is used in various rites and appears as part of the Khalsa symbol.
Khitan (I)	The Muslim rite of circumcision.
Khwan (B)	The Buddhist spirit which looks after, and over, the life of an individual.
Kiddush (J)	Literally means the sanctification of the day. A prayer recited by Jews over a glass of wine.
Kirpan (S)	A curved dagger worn as one of the 5 K's, the external symbols of being a Sikh.
Kosher (J)	Food which has been permitted and prepared according to Jewish law.
Langar (S)	The kitchen or eating area where all Sikhs, and non-Sikhs, are welcomed to share a free meal together.
Laws of Manu (H)	Describes the origins of the Hindu caste system together with its rights and duties.

Lent (C)	A 40 day period of reflection, prayer and penance prior to Easter.
Mahabharata (H)	A Hindu epic poem. Commences with the words known as the Bhagavad Gita.
Mohel (J)	The name given to a trained circumcisor who performs the Jewish ceremony of Brit Milah.
Mool Mantra (S)	In essence the central credal statement of Sikhism, declaring the nature and unity of God.
Muhammad (I)	Key figure in Islam (lived 570–632 CE). Believed by Muslims to be the final prophet through whom Allah revealed His truth.
Nonconformist (C)	Following religious toleration in 1689, a group known as freechurchmen or dissenters emerged. Today these are called Nonconformists and describe any who do not conform to the established Church, which in the UK is the Anglican or Church of England.
Om (H)	The holiest Hindu name for God, symbolising the Absolute.
Pali (B)	The language of the Theravada Buddhist scriptures. It is also considered to be the language of the Buddha. The scriptures are the orally preserved teachings of the Buddha and his disciples.
Pandit (H)	A person who is learned and wise. Often used as a point of reference by Hindu families.
Patka (S)	A fairly tightly fitting head-covering for Sikhs with room on the top for the uncut hair to be kept in place. Also sometimes worn under the turban. Worn by children and adults.
Pesach (J)	A term meaning Passover. Festival celebrating the ten plagues and the subsequent exodus from Egypt.
Peter's Vision	Full account in Acts chapter 10, which many believe abolished the Jewish dietary restrictions for the Christian.
Purim (J)	Festival based on the book of Esther, the heroine who delivered the Jews from possible death.
Qur'an (I)	Literally means 'recitation'. The name given to the sacred writings of Islam. Written in Arabic.
Rajasic (H)	One of the three qualities, according to Hindus, which determine the characteristic of any material being.
Ramadhan (I)	The Muslim month set aside for fasting from food and drink during daylight hours.
Ramayana (H)	Hindu epic poem forming part of scriptures. Tells story of Rama and Sita, remembered at Diwali festival.

Rosh Hashanah (J)	Jewish New Year festival.
Rosh Hodesh (J)	A celebration linked to the New Moon, used as a means of adjusting the lunar/solar calendar.
Rumalah (S)	The name given to the elegant cloth used to cover the Guru Granth Sahib. Sikhs give these as gifts to God. They are given to Sikhs at significant events in their lives such as birthdays or marriage.
Sadvic (H)	One of the three qualities which Hindus believe determine the characteristic of any material being.
Sahaj Path (S)	Similar to the Akhand Path though not a continuous reading but spread over seven days.
Salah (I)	The five compulsory daily prayers.
Sandek (J)	The Jewish Godparent who on the eighth day of a boy's life will hold the baby at the Brit Milah ceremony.
Sangha (B)	Those who have formally and ritually renounced their former lives and become Buddhist monks or bhikkhus accepting the discipline that entails. Often the term is used for the community of monks.
Sawm (I)	One of the Five Pillars of Islam, it is the obligatory fast during the daylight hours of the month of Ramadhan.
Schechita (J)	Jewish ritual slaughter of animals.
Seder (J)	The name given to the meal at Passover. The term means 'order' as the meal follows careful traditional pattern.
Sephardic (J)	The term given to those Jews and their descendents originally expelled from the Iberian Peninsular in the C15.
Seudat Mitzvah (plural mitzvoth) (J)	Seudat Mitzvah is the rejoicing around a commandment. It is therefore a ritual celebration.
Shabbat (J)	The seventh day of the week, commencing sunset on Friday until sunset on Saturday. Holy day for the Jews, which commemorates the final day of the creation when God rested.
Shahadah (I)	The declaration of faith.
Shema (J)	Important scriptural affirmation of God's unity and human responsibility towards Him.
Simnel Cake (C)	Rich fruit cake which is eaten by Christians during Lent or at Easter.
Singh (S)	The name given to all Sikh males meaning 'lion'. It may not be used by those not initiated. It is always used by those initiated.
Smriti (H)	Term meaning 'memory', applied to those Hindu scriptures which have been passed on from memory. They are to be distinguished from those which were revealed by God.

Sruti (H)	Hindu scriptures which are divinely revealed, as distinguished from those which are transmitted via human memory.
Sunna (I)	Means 'traditions', and reflects that which is practised by Muslims, based on the example of the Prophet Muhammad (pbuh).
Sutras (H)	Sayings which are designed to guide Hindus in matters of morality and spirituality.
Tahneek (I)	An unusual Muslim ceremony in the UK, when honey is placed in the mouth of a newly born baby.
Talmud (J)	Second in authority to the Torah, these writings are the rabbinic traditions recorded before the end of the fifth century CE.
Tenach (J)	The Hebrew Bible with its three sections: Law, Writings and the Prophets.
Thamasic (H)	One of the three qualities which for Hindus determine the characteristic of any material being.
Torah (J)	Generally a term meaning teaching. In a narrower sense it refers to the five books of Moses, also called the Pentateuch. These are Genesis, Exodus, Leviticus, Numbers and Deuteronomy.
Tripitaka (B)	The name literally means the 'three baskets', and these three sections form the scriptures for those of the Theravada Buddhist tradition.
Upanayana (H)	The term used for the Sacred Thread ceremony for the young Brahmin boy.
Upanishads (H)	The last section of the Vedas. They are concerned with discussing the nature of human existence.
Uposatha (H)	Term applied by Hindus to the days midway through the lunar fortnight. Analogous to the Jewish sabbath or Christian Sunday in terms of importance.
Vak or Hukam (S)	The equivalent of the Christian 'verse for the day', which has been selected at random from the Guru Granth Sahib. It is often displayed on the noticeboard at the Gurdwara for the lay community to see and meditate upon.
Vedas (H)	The most ancient and sacred Hindu scriptures, they are sruti. There are four main vedas.
Wan Pra (B)	Term given to the four monthly prayer days within the Buddhist lunar calendar. Observed by the lay community.
Zakat (I)	One of the Five Pillars of Islam, this Pillar is an obligatory act of almsgiving. It may amount to 2.5 per cent of a person's savings, which is then given to the poor.

Index

Abishekam 11
Adi Granth 55
Adult baptism 9
Agreed Syllabus 19
Ahimsa 23
Akhand Path 16, 56, 69, 70
Angel of Death 14
Aqeeqah 13
Arabic 51
Ark 54
Artanai 11
Artefacts 73
  Buddhist 74–5
  Christian 76
  Hindu 77
  Islamic 79
  Jewish 80
  Sikh 81
Ashkenazi 14, 54,
Azan 12

Bhikkus 7, 20
Bible Society 49
Birth rites 5–17
Bismillah 26
Brahmin 10, 37, 38, 39
Brit Milah 14

Calendars 58
  Buddhist 58–60
  Christian 61–2
  Hindu 63–4

Islamic 64–5
Jewish 66–7
Sikh 68–70
Central Statistical Office 3
Chism 8
Christening 8
Church 8, 75
Clothing 34
  Buddhist 34–5
  Christian 35–6
  Hindu 36–9
  Islamic 39–40
  Jewish 40–1
  Sikh 42–4
Creed 50
Customs 73
  Buddhist 74–5
  Christian 75–6
  Hindu 76–8
  Islamic 78–9
  Jewish 80
  Sikh 80–1

Dasam Granth 56
Diet 19
  Buddhist 19–21
  Christian 21–3
  Hindu 23–6
  Islamic 26–8
  Jewish 28–30
  Sikh 30–2
Diwali 26

Easter 23
Education Reform Act 1988 1, 19, 86
Eucharist 22

Family unit 3
Fasting 22, 25, 27, 78
Five K's 17, 32, 42, 81
Five Pillars 27, 52, 53, 78
Four Noble Truths 48

Gayatri Mantra 38
Golden Rule 85
Grace 21, 30
Granthi 17
Gregorian 61
Gupurbs 68, 70
Gurdwara 15, 16, 17, 31-2, 42, 43, 56, 57, 68, 81
Guru Arjan 55, 68, 69
Guru Gobind Singh 15, 31, 56, 69
Guru Granth Sahib 16, 17, 30, 31, 55, 56, 68, 69
Guru Nanak 31, 55, 68
Guru Teg Bahadur 68

Hadith 26, 39, 53
Haggadah 30
Hajji 39
Halal/haram 27
Hannukah 30, 80
Hijab 40
Hijrah 64
Humanism 3, 83-6

Id ul Adha 28
Id ul Fitr 27, 40
Ikons 76

Jehovah Witnesses 3, 86-7

Kaccha 44, 81
Kameez 37, 42
Kangha 43
Kara 17, 44
Kara Prashad 17
Karma 23
Kaur 15
Kesh 42
Khanda 17
Khitan 13
Khwan 6
Kiddush 15, 29
Kirpan 17, 32, 44
Kittel 41
Kosher 28, 80

Langar 17, 30
Language of religion 46
   Buddhist 46-8
   Christian 48-50
   Hindu 50-1
   Islamic 51-4
   Jewish 54-5
   Sikh 55-7
Lent 22-3

Menorah 80
Mohel 15
Mool Mantra 17, 55
Mosque 27, 79

Names 5-6
   Buddhist 6-7
   Christian 7-9
   Hindu 9-11
   Islamic 11-13
   Jewish 13-15
   Sikh 15-17

Naming Rites 5-6
   Buddhist 6-7

Christian 7–9
Hindu 9–11
Islamic 11–13
Jewish 13–15
Sikh 15–17
Nihansingh 31–2
Noble Eightfold Path 19, 48

Om 10, 39

Parshad see Karah Prasad
Patka 43
Pesach (Passover) 30, 41, 80
Phyllactery 80
Pitaka 47, 48
Puja 24, 77
Purim 13, 30

Qur'an 11, 12, 26, 39, 51, 52, 53, 78, 79

Ramadhan 27, 40, 66, 78
Rosh Hashanah 30, 66
Rosh Hodesh 66
Rumalah 17, 56

Sahaj Path 16
Salah 78
Samskara 11
Sandek 14
Sangha 7, 20, 21, 47, 74
Sawm 78
Seder 30, 41, 80
Sephardic 14, 54
Seudat Mitzvah 15
Shabbat 14, 29, 41, 80
Shahadah 53, 78
Shalwar 37, 42
Shariah 78–9
Shema 54–5, 80

Singh 15
Smriti 51
Sruti 51
Sunna 53, 78
Sutras 48
Synagogue 14, 55, 80

Talmud 54
Tefillin 41
Temple 11, 20, 24, 25, 34–5, 37, 47, 59, 74, 77
Tenach 54
Torah 13, 14, 28, 29, 40, 41, 54, 66
Tripitaka 47, 48
Turban 42, 43

Upanayana 37
Upanishads 51
Uposatha 59

Visiting places of worship
  Buddhist 74–5
  Christian 75–6
  Hindu 77–8
  Islamic 79
  Jewish 80
  Sikh 81

Wan Pra 35, 59
Wat 74
Watchtower 86
Westernising influences 2, 9, 12, 31, 32, 38, 40, 59

Yamelkah 41, 80
Yom Kippur 41

Zakat 27, 78